JESUS,
MAKE ME
Fully Alive

"Each day, Jesus calls out to our hearts to sit with him, and this book is the perfect companion for those intimate moments . . . our Holy Hours."

Maclaine Noah
Creator of A Catholic Convo

"Fr. Tim Anastos's book is an excellent resource for college students and other young adults to begin to encounter the Lord in daily prayer. It would be a meaningful gift for high school or college graduates to help them stay grounded in their faith."

Most Rev. Robert Barron
Bishop of Winona–Rochester

"Fr. Anastos has given us a resource that is concise, readable, and packed with wisdom. Anyone struggling with a commitment to prayer or understanding the Eucharist will benefit from this guidebook!"

Jackie and Bobby Angel
Catholic speakers, authors, and YouTubers

"The idea of praying a holy hour can seem daunting or even scary. 'You want me to do what?' But Fr. Anastos breaks down this game-changing practice in such an easy, gentle, and approachable way that you'll be stoked to go pray. A holy hour has never felt so doable."

Tanner Kalina
Catholic evangelist

JESUS, MAKE ME
Fully Alive

30 Holy Hour
Reflections

FR. TIM ANASTOS

Ave Maria Press · AVE · Notre Dame, Indiana

Scripture texts in this work are taken from the *New American Bible, revised edition* © 2010, 1991, 1986, 1970 Confraternity of Christian Doctrine, Washington, DC, and are used by permission of the copyright owner. All Rights Reserved. No part of the *New American Bible* may be reproduced in any form without permission in writing from the copyright owner.

Nihil Obstat: Reverend Monsignor Michael Heintz, PhD
  Censor Librorum

Imprimatur: Most Reverend Kevin C. Rhoades
  Bishop of Fort Wayne–South Bend
  Given at Fort Wayne, Indiana, on September 19, 2023

Excerpt on pages 161–162 from *The Ave Treasury of Catholic Prayers*, ©2023 by Ave Maria Press, is used with the permission of the publisher.

Foreword © 2023 by Most Rev. Andrew H. Cozzens

Founded in 1865, Ave Maria Press is a ministry of the United States Province of Holy Cross.

www.avemariapress.com

Paperback: ISBN-13 978-1-64680-299-9

E-book: ISBN-13 978-1-64680-300-2

Cover image © Maria Oswalt/Unsplash.com.

Cover and text design by Andy Wagoner.

Printed and bound in the United States of America.

Library of Congress Cataloging-in-Publication Data is available.

To my amazing '22–'23 Newman Cor Team:
Becca, Fidel, Lauren, Anthony, Emmy, Mary,
and Chanelle, for inspiring me to write this

To Bishop Austin Vetter for teaching
me how to pray

CONTENTS

FOREWORD

Throughout my years as a priest and bishop, especially in my work in youth ministry, it has been my privilege to witness over and over the tremendous power of Christ's presence in the Eucharist, especially in inviting young people to spend time in Eucharistic Adoration (or Holy Hour devotion). I have often seen that when people come before the Lord with an open heart in adoration, he begins to speak to them deeply of his love and often brings about great healing. No matter what is happening in your life—whether you want to conquer an embedded personal weakness, seek healing from some physical or emotional wound, or simply encounter Jesus in daily life—this book will show you how to make the most of the time you spend in Eucharistic Adoration. Step by step, you will discover how to receive the graces you need and the answers you seek.

Whenever we place ourselves in the presence of the Lord, he invites us to speak to him freely and without fear. We can ask the hard questions and wait expectantly for the answers. As Fr. Tim points out in this practical spiritual resource, whenever we show up, Jesus is already there, waiting.

This sense of Jesus's presence in the Eucharist has always been very real to me personally, and it profoundly affected my sense of vocation. When I was much younger, serving at Mass, I would kneel close to the altar and sense Jesus's presence. As I grew, I knew I wanted to live close to Jesus in the Blessed Sacrament, and this was the beginning of my priestly vocation. Eventually I realized he was calling me to dedicate my life to the Eucharist. For many years I have made a daily Holy Hour the center of my prayer life. I find this time in silent adoration essential to my relationship with him.

I love the way St. John Paul described his own ordination when he said, "I was ordained a servant of the Eucharist." The Mass is the source and summit of our lives, and spending time in adoration helps us come to the Mass ready to offer and receive all the Lord has to give. In the Eucharist we discover our identity. We are the bride of Christ, his beloved to whom he wants to give himself. We are also the Body of Christ; as we become one with him, he wants to live his life in us. When we encounter Jesus in the Eucharist and allow ourselves to be drawn deeper into his heart, it also changes how we see ourselves (our identity) and our sense of purpose (our mission). It becomes easier to stand against the trials and temptations of the world and to refrain from falling into the trap of measuring our sense of worth by our accomplishments—what we do.

Perhaps you are holding this book in your hands right now because you are looking for that same kind of encounter. Perhaps your prayer, too, is, "Jesus, make me fully alive." "Jesus, show me who I am to you." "Jesus, heal me!" "Jesus, show me the purpose of my life." As you follow the advice of Fr. Tim and take up the challenge of spending time with Jesus in a regular Holy Hour, entering into dialogue with the One who is waiting for you, you will discover One who already knows everything there is to know about you yet loves you more than you will ever comprehend. Learning to make a regular Holy Hour in the presence of the Blessed Sacrament will change your life profoundly. This spiritual guide will help you to rekindle a fire in your own heart so that you in turn can take up the call to share his love with our world. St. John Paul II, Pope Benedict, and Pope Francis have all spoken about the need to spend time in adoration in order to fully receive the gift of the Eucharist. As Pope Francis said, "Only in adoration, only in the presence of the Lord, do we truly rediscover our taste and passion for evangelization."[1]

It is no secret that we live in difficult times when many people have lost the sense of God and his presence in our world. This is why the US Conference of Catholic Bishops called in 2021 for a National Eucharistic Revival. The Eucharist is the greatest gift we have in the Church because it contains Christ and the gift of himself on the Cross. We need to rediscover the incredible gift of Christ in the Eucharist. I am grateful to Fr. Tim for answering the call to become a Eucharistic preacher during the National Eucharistic Revival. At a time when so many have neglected or forgotten the transforming power of the Eucharist, we need more young men and women to take their place in the great procession of the faithful, who will draw those who most need the healing consolation of the Holy Spirit back into the heart of the Church. Let us pray for each other that we will be faithful to our calling and that this book, which has already blessed so many, will continue to bear fruit for the kingdom of God.

Bishop Andrew H. Cozzens
Diocese of Crookston, Minnesota
Chairman of the USCCB National Eucharistic Revival

AUTHOR'S NOTE

Friends, thank you so much for your desire to go deeper with the Lord. Prayer is the absolute lifeblood of our faith. Your desire to pray is the first step toward greater holiness. I have personally seen a thirst for prayer among my college students on campus, which is where the origins of this book came from. (If you are a bit older, thank you for picking up this book anyway! I want to apologize in advance if any of these cultural references aren't especially relatable, and thank you for your lived example of what it means to be fully alive in faith!

As I said, I have written this book primarily for young people, who are constantly bombarded with more noise, more screens, and more anxiety and as a result have a greater desire for more silence, prayer, and intimacy. These amazing spiritual gifts may be found when you intentionally spend time with Jesus—the Way, the Truth, and the Life—in each Holy Hour (adoration). No matter how old you are, you were made for this kind of joy-filled encounter. Don't be anxious about what will happen or worry about what you will say. Just come and open your heart to what Jesus wants to say to you. You were made for this!

Fr. Tim

INTRODUCTION

In 2016, my best priest friends (BPFs) and I went on a short vacay to Southern California. Toward the end of our time there, late one evening, sirens began to wail across Laguna Beach, and we watched a whole army of cop cars and SWAT vans drive down the coast to one of the hotels. There may have been helicopters as well. Bottom line: something crazy and dangerous was going down in the heart of SoCal.

I remember being worried about a horrible crime or loss of life that may have taken place. I said a few prayers for the possible victims in that situation and then went to bed. The next morning my BPFs and I found out what crazy thing had happened the previous night, and it was more horrific and sinister than I possibly could have imagined:

Someone had broken into Justin Bieber's hotel room.

A Bieber fangirl (a Belieber) snuck into the hotel where Justin Bieber was staying, found out his room number, and somehow made it into his hotel room (where she was quickly subdued by Bieber's personal bodyguards). The whole time, the fangirl acted as if she and Bieber were good friends! She didn't act crazy or out of control. She acted as if what she was doing was normal. The fangirl seriously believed that she was supposed to be there!

How did she get to this point? I imagine this fangirl listened to Justin Bieber's albums over and over and over. Maybe she went to several of his concerts; maybe she even spent extra money for a backstage pass. She could have scoured YouTube for interviews of Bieber, learning everything she could about his personality and life story. By getting to know him at a distance, the fangirl could have begun thinking that her relationship with Justin was real. Listening to his lyrics, she could have imagined that he understood her, too. But the stark reality is that he did not know her. Their "friendship" was entirely one-sided and imaginary.

To be honest, some of us do this with Jesus, too! We go to Mass all the time, pray before meals, and give up things during Lent, but we do those things at a distance. In our minds we think, "Oh yeah, Jesus loves me! Me and him—we're tight!"

But is that reality? Do I really know Jesus? Have I spent time with him? The last thing we want is to get to heaven and find out we didn't know the real Jesus, like the Belieber fangirl who walked into Justin's hotel room and was immediately seen as an imposter.

When I arrive in heaven, will I immediately be seen as an imposter?

If this is resonating at all with your heart, don't be afraid! The good news is Jesus Christ gave us an all-access pass to him! We have access through the Church, the sacraments (starting with our baptism), and prayer.

You don't have to fear being an imposter. Jesus desperately wants you to know him. All you have to do is go to him and spend time with him in prayer. This is what the saints have done throughout the history of the Church. Today, this prayer practice is known as adoration or "the Holy Hour."

HOW DO I MAKE A HOLY HOUR?

I made my first "official" Holy Hour when I was a sophomore in college. One evening in the fall, I went to an Irish pub on campus for a Bible study with a few juniors. After a great Bible study, the juniors invited me to the Newman Center chapel to pray a Holy Hour with them. I had heard of "making a Holy Hour" before but was never invited to do it. So I followed along.

For the next hour we prayed together, and in all honesty it was the worst Holy Hour of my entire life (so far). I acted as if I knew what I was doing, but I had no clue! I was too prideful to ask any of the junior guys for help or guidance. Also my mind was racing the entire time, thinking about upcoming exams and relationship drama. The only time I may have actually prayed was when I said one Our Father . . . I even opened up the worship aid in the pew and read through song lyrics at random.

Yes, my first "official" Holy Hour was a hot mess.

I made my first "unofficial" Holy Hour when I was a junior in high school. On a Friday night in the spring, thirty classmates and I finished a powerful retreat in our high school chapel. Everyone, including myself, was on a "spiritual high." From what everyone was saying, it had been redeeming and healing for all of us. As we left the high school, I realized I had forgotten my hoodie, so I went back into the school—to the chapel—to get it.

Inside, the chapel was dark except for two lights over the altar, and I had an overwhelming urge to stay with God. After having a fruitful retreat, my heart was full of joy and gratitude. I just wanted to stay with the Lord a little longer. So I sat down and stayed with him. Without realizing it, I spent around an hour in the chapel. During that time, I talked to Jesus, thanked Jesus, prayed in silence, and shared my upcoming week with Jesus. Despite breaking the rules and being in the high school after hours, it was one of the quickest hours of my life.

God is so good. I made a Holy Hour before I even knew what a Holy Hour was!

Notice the differences between my first "official" Holy Hour and my first "unofficial" Holy Hour. It is probably obvious which example you would prefer to experience. But I would argue that they were both good Holy Hours. In both examples two things happened:

1. I showed up.

2. Jesus was present, loving me.

When it comes to prayer in general, the first and most important thing you have to do is show up. Then the Lord, who is always present, will never stop loving you. Remember, this is your relationship with Jesus! There will be Holy Hours that suck because you're distracted or you can't hear the Lord speak to you, and there will be incredible Holy Hours that will rock your socks and open up a whole new part of your heart. All you need to do is show up.

Wherever you are in your journey with Christ, don't be afraid. The Holy Hour is supposed to be not intimidating but rather completely normal and for everyone. We make a Holy

Hour any time we *intentionally spend time with Jesus in his Eucharistic presence.* That's it!

Did you know that Jesus desires to spend time with you? It's true! Just like any relationship or friendship that we have in our lives, we need to spend time to grow in relationship, love, knowledge, and trust. Imagine if you hung out with your best friend for an hour or less on Sunday and then ghosted them for the rest of the week until the following Sunday. That would be pretty unhealthy! In the same way, if we spend one hour on Sunday at Mass and then ghost Jesus for the rest of the week . . . that's not much of a relationship. So the Church, in its wisdom, encourages us *to intentionally spend time with Jesus, who is waiting for us in the tabernacle.*

Let's break this down:

Intentionally: When we are intentional, we are deliberate in our thoughts and actions. We deeply care about living purposely with our goals. It's easy to be intentional with the things that we care about: our friendships, money, and family. It's easier to become a bit careless or even reckless with the things we don't care about. Think about it—how intentional are you with your sleep, studying, and diet? We don't care as much about those things.

We are called to be intentional with our relationship with Jesus. To be intentional with Jesus is to live on purpose, have direction and focus, and strive to make the most of our time and energy in pursuit of Christ.

Spending Time: Spoiler alert . . . Jesus is real. Not only is Jesus real, but also he is alive. He is living now! So the way that we can grow in a relationship with him is to spend time with him in the present moment. Making a Holy Hour is carving out time to be with him. Later we'll talk about the details of what that looks like, but we actually have to offer Jesus our time.

With Jesus: Our modern, secular culture teaches us about mindfulness and meditation. But prayer is different. Prayer

is communication with a person. Mindfulness and meditation look inward at oneself and can become a lonely self-help
exercise. While mindfulness and meditation can sometimes
help with stress, these practices also empty out our thoughts,
emotions, and desires. This "emptying" is directly opposed to
prayer. After you spend time with a friend, you are more alive,
not "emptied out." Prayer is not emptying out but rather pouring in. Jesus Christ pours his love and grace into our hearts
and makes us more alive.

   In the Tabernacle (or Monstrance): Notice that little light at
the front of the church? It is an invitation to stop what we are
doing and experience an encounter with Jesus. Just as the ark
of the covenant, housed in the Holy of Holies in the Temple,
was the place God dwelt with his people, so the tabernacle
is a place where heaven touches earth and Christ fulfills his
promise never to leave or forsake us.

   Just begin where you are right now. Are you ready to cul-
tivate a daily or weekly "Holy Hour habit"? This book will
help you. Do you want to spend just a few moments with Jesus
during your parish's established Eucharistic devotion schedule? No problem—he's happy to see you! You can visit Jesus
any time the consecrated host is placed in a monstrance, or
consecrated hosts are reserved inside the tabernacle (the ornate
box usually displayed behind the altar). All you have to do is
show up!

The Question That Started It All

When it comes to the real origin of the Holy Hour, we look to
none other than Jesus himself. Throughout the gospels, Jesus
is always going back to be with his Father. Taking about five
minutes to skim the gospels, I counted ten separate instances
where Jesus goes off by himself to pray and be with the Father.
Jesus recognized his identity as a beloved Son. He was rooted

in that reality when he went off to pray. When we go to prayer, we are going to the Father who reminds us of who we are: his beloved sons and daughters. The Holy Hour is having the privilege to participate in what Jesus held most important in his life on earth.

Now, the question that started it all, that breathes the Holy Hour into existence, is Jesus's words to Peter and the apostles in Matthew 26:40: "When he returned to his disciples, he found them asleep. He said to Peter, 'So you could not keep watch with me for one hour?'" Jesus, after giving himself to the apostles at the Last Supper, goes with his apostles to the garden of Gethsemane to pray. Jesus goes off alone to pray but desires that his apostles stay awake and keep vigil. After heart-wrenching prayer with the Father, knowing his Passion is close, he goes back to his apostles and finds them asleep.

Again, what Jesus held most important during his life on earth was his relationship with the Father. During this scene in the garden, Jesus invites his closest friends into the relationship that he has with his Father. Every time you intentionally enter into prayer, Jesus is inviting you into that most special relationship! But when Jesus finds the apostles asleep, he says to Peter, "So you could not keep watch with me for one hour?" Jesus doesn't accuse him, and he doesn't try to guilt Peter. Jesus gently asks the question that reveals his heart: he desired for them to be in relationship with the Father, but he would never force them. Jesus desires desperately for you to be a part of his relationship with his dad, but he will never force you. He gently invites you. Making a Holy Hour is saying yes to the invitation.

The OG Influencer

Archbishop Fulton Sheen was a Catholic bishop and theologian in the mid-1900s. He was, in my opinion, the OG (that is, original) social media influencer. As a bishop, Sheen became a popular TV personality, sharing the Catholic faith in an engaging and lively way. He gained millions of "followers" around the country when he began hosting his own show, *Life Is Worth Living.*

During my senior year of college, everyone at the Newman Center was reading books by Sheen, so I was introduced to his autobiography, *Treasure in Clay.* In it, he describes how his life was changed when he began to make a Holy Hour before the Blessed Sacrament. About his experience making a Holy Hour he said,

> No one in the world could interfere with that hour of silence and communion with the Almighty. During that hour, I would try to focus my mind on the most high God, in the hope that He would teach me something of the mystery of His love. . . . The Holy Hour became like an oxygen tank to revive the breath of the Holy Spirit in the midst of the foul and fetid atmosphere of the world.[1]

I remember reading that and saying to myself, "Right? The world brings me down. I feel crappy without the Lord . . . I need more time with Jesus!" Sheen's words about Holy Hours enlivened something in my heart, made me crave more time with Jesus. It definitely wasn't an hour at first, but I knew I had to spend time with Jesus if I really wanted to be lifted out of the negative and heavy culture that I was living in.

I am not the only one inspired by Sheen to start praying more. He has inspired hundreds of thousands of Catholics in the same way. Mid-1900s to now, the increased practice of the Holy Hour is in large part due to Archbishop Sheen's invitation to the world to take their spiritual lives more seriously. To Sheen, the Holy Hour wasn't a magical formula that a person had to "accomplish" to be holy but rather the expression of a lived-out relationship. One of the reasons so many of my friends at the Newman Center enjoyed reading Sheen was because it was obvious he was in love. It's the same vibe you get whenever you talk with an engaged friend about their fiancé. This person's obviously in love. The more time we spend with the Beloved, the more we become like him. Archbishop Sheen wanted to share an easy way for the people of God to grow in intimacy.

> The purpose of the Holy Hour is to encourage deep and personal encounter with Christ. The holy and glorious God is constantly inviting us to come to Him, to converse with Him, to ask for such things as we need and to experience what a blessing there is in fellowship with Him.[2]

Other Influencers of the Holy Hour

Just as Archbishop Sheen popularized the Holy Hour for the modern Church, many saints before him encouraged the faithful in this practice. In the eighteenth century, St. Alphonsus Liguori wrote extensively on Eucharistic devotion before the Blessed Sacrament. He encouraged the faithful to make time for daily prayer to really know Our Lord.

> Certainly, among all devotions after that of receiving the Sacraments, that of adoring Jesus in the Blessed Sacrament holds first place, is the most pleasing to God and the most useful to ourselves.[3]

In the nineteenth century, St. John Bosco dedicated his life to caring for young boys and girls in Italy's school system. He perpetually encouraged his students to spend time with Jesus in prayer before the Blessed Sacrament.

St. Maximilian Kolbe, one of my favorite saints, had a deep devotion to the Holy Hour. His daily Holy Hour was the central part of his day in his life as a Franciscan friar in Poland. During one of his Holy Hours, Kolbe had a profound and well-known experience with Our Lady. As he prayed, Mary came to him and offered him two crowns: one white and the other red. She asked Kolbe if he would accept the white crown of purity or the red crown of martyrdom. Like a boss, he chose both!

It was through his daily Holy Hours that Kolbe drew closer and closer to Jesus and Mary and became more and more alive. Later in his life, when Kolbe was imprisoned at Auschwitz, he continued his commitment to his Holy Hour. He found creative ways to spend time in prayer and encouraged the prisoners around him to pray as well. The Eucharist and the Holy Hour were his strength and comfort during his inhumane imprisonment.

St. Teresa of Calcutta is another example of someone who was so in love with Christ and kept a commitment to the Holy Hour every day. She and her sisters spent at least an hour in prayer every day as part of their rule of life. Still today, the Missionaries of Charity established by Mother Teresa spend an hour each day before the Blessed Sacrament to strengthen them for their work.

In his talk during the FOCUS Seek conference, Jason Evert, a famous Catholic chastity speaker, evangelist, and writer, talked about Mother Teresa's devotion to her Holy Hour. He told the story of two Missionaries of Charity who told Mother Teresa that they didn't think it was possible to do a Holy Hour that day because they had too much to do. Mother Teresa calmly told them to go and do two Holy Hours!

This mentality is what helped Olympic swimmer and twenty-three-time gold medalist Michael Phelps to be so successful. Phelps, whenever he was performing subpar, would train twice a day and for longer periods of time. He doubled down on his efforts and focused on the goal. Mother Teresa would similarly double down on the "relationship" before "the mission." She knew it was more important for the sisters to root their identity in Jesus, and not in their work. The Holy Hour roots us in our identity and then prepares us for mission.

Lastly, our three most recent popes have been great advocates of the practice of the Holy Hour. Pope Francis has made the Holy Hour a regular part of his daily schedule, saying, "We have lost the sense of adoration: we must regain it, starting with us, consecrated people."[4] He continues to encourage the Church to spend time in adoration. In a moving meeting with religious sisters, Pope Francis said,

> I urge you to devote yourselves in particular to prayer of adoration: this is important . . . it is beautiful to worship in silence before the Blessed Sacrament, to be in the consoling presence of Jesus.[5]

Pope Benedict XVI wrote extensively on the importance of intentional prayer before the Blessed Sacrament. In his apostolic exhortation (letter) *Sacramentum Caritatis*, the Holy Father wrote, "Through the sacrament of the Eucharist Jesus draws the faithful into his 'hour'; he shows us the bond that he willed to establish between himself and us, between his own person and the Church."[6]

Lastly, St. John Paul II was devoted wholeheartedly to making a daily Holy Hour. He famously stated in his encyclical *Ecclesia de Eucharistia* (*On the Eucharist and Its Relationship to the Church*),

> The worship of the Eucharist outside of the Mass is of inestimable value for the life of the Church. This worship is strictly linked to the celebration of the Eucharistic Sacrifice . . . It is pleasant to spend time with him, to lie close to his breast like the Beloved Disciple and to feel the infinite love present in his heart. If in our time Christians must be distinguished above all by the "art of prayer," how can we not feel a renewed need to spend time in spiritual converse, in

silent adoration, in heartfelt love before Christ present in the Most Holy Sacrament?[8]

I know several older priests who witnessed St. John Paul II praying his Holy Hour at the Vatican. They all described it similarly that during St. John Paul II's time of prayer, nothing else mattered. The beautiful realization is that it's totally reciprocal! Whenever you go into prayer, for Jesus Christ, nothing else matters. In your Holy Hour, *you* are the center of his gaze.

How to Make a Holy Hour

Now that we understand the origins and the "why" of the Holy Hour, we can get to the practical details of what you actually do there. For those who may be thinking, "Finally! Just tell me how to do the Holy Hour!" please remember that the Holy Hour is about relationship. It's personal. There is no right or wrong way of relating your heart to Jesus. However, by pulling from the rich history of spirituality within the Church, the words of the saints, and meaningful passages of scripture, and mixing in the helpful guidelines and tips from this book, you can make your Holy Hour even more effective and fruitful.

Time

The term *Holy Hour* can be deceiving. You can make a Holy Hour even if you have just thirty minutes or so. Traditionally, yes, a Holy Hour is an hour. But remember, Holy Hour is defined as intentionally spending time with Jesus. So, depending on your state in life—married, single, student—you may not have the time to intentionally spend a whole hour with him. And Jesus doesn't want you to put it off until you do! Just start by offering what time you have and let it grow naturally over time.

Pray about what amount of time the Lord is asking you to give him. Be as generous as you can—even when you are busy, you can give him more than five or ten minutes! To get the most out of this book, commit to spending at least thirty minutes. That's not a lot of time—think about the amount of time you have spent with people you don't even like very much or the time you waste during a scrolling session on social media. Intimacy is not found in any friendship or spousal relationship in ten minutes a day. Time is precious to us. It is something we protect and covet. For our thirty-day journey, thirty minutes is the bare minimum amount of time that the Lord of the Universe deserves!

Place

Location matters! Jesus says in Matthew 6:6, "But when you pray, go to your inner room, close the door, and pray to your Father in secret. And your Father who sees in secret will repay you." Where is the most effective place for you to spend intimate time with the Lord? Silence and intimacy can be challenging. We are distracted and disconnected from our ability to pray. We are bombarded with constant noise and stimulation from social media and technology. Sometimes we need several minutes to detox from noise before even being able to pray. This is why location is important.

For obvious reasons, spending time before the tabernacle in adoration of the Blessed Sacrament is the very best way to make a Holy Hour. Going to adoration is like being in front of a nuclear reactor—you can't feel anything, but the radiation is slowly changing you at an atomic level. In adoration, you may not feel anything, but the *radiating* love of Jesus Christ is transforming you. Of course, Jesus is present wherever we pray, from the bathroom to the classroom, but there is no better place to experience the true and substantial presence of the risen Lord than in adoration. So, if there is an adoration chapel close by, or a parish that offers adoration, please consider this as your place to make your Holy Hour.

If a church or adoration chapel is not a possibility for you, consider creating a space within your home that can be dedicated for prayer. If you have a crucifix, sacred icon, or image that helps you to enter into prayer, add it to your space. No matter if it's a room or a little nook, create a place that is different from where you work and play. Your brain needs it! If we pray in the same place long enough, we develop a habit where our bodies easily move into "prayer mode."

Silence

I experienced the power of silence for the first time as a kid when I watched *The Lion King*. In the movie, there's an emotional scene where Simba finds his father Mufasa's dead body. During the scene, there is no dialogue or music. I remember as a kid feeling intense emotion during the silence. It was the first time I ever thought, "Wow, there's something different about silence."

In *The Power of Silence*, Cardinal Robert Sarah wrote, "Silence is not an absence. On the contrary, it is the manifestation of a presence, the most intense of all presences. Silence is not an emptiness, but a plenitude, a totality in which I encounter myself, and in which I encounter the loving God who created me."[9] Bottom line, silence is a huge grace and helps us to encounter God!

Part of making a Holy Hour is embracing the silence and growing to listen for Jesus in the silence. In 2011, Pope Benedict XVI spoke about the importance of silence when creating an "oasis" for the spirit:

> God speaks in silence, but we need to know how to listen. If we are constantly talking, how can we hear God's voice? In silence, we are better able to perceive and contemplate God's great works, which is why the most authentic religious experience is often linked to monasteries and

hermitages, where people withdraw from the noise of the world in order to make space for God.[10]

In the silence of each Holy Hour, we make space for God to speak to us. It might feel awkward the first few times you make your Holy Hour since we have noise around us all the time. Be honest with Jesus about it. Jesus spent forty days alone in the desert for you. He is the master of being in silence. Ask him to teach you. Tell him that you want to hear him. Share with Jesus your desire to fall in love with silence.

Brutal Honesty

"Fine." That was my most-used word during my high school years. I would come home, grab a snack, and my mom would ask me, "How was your day?"

"Fine," I would respond.

Then my dad would come home and ask me, "Hey, little buddy, how was your day?"

"Fine," I would say.

When my dad would pick me up after tennis practice, he'd ask me in the car, "So, how was practice?"

And sure enough, I would say, "Fine."

I look back on those years and regret not opening up to my parents and sharing what was actually going on in my heart. I was guarding myself from feeling too many emotions and trying to solve all of my high school drama on my own. In the same way, we can guard our hearts when we approach God in prayer, telling Jesus that we're "fine" and that he's "fine."

We can do this at Mass, too. We say, "Lord, I'm not worthy that you should enter under my roof," but do we really mean it? Or are we brushing off what is going on, going through the motions as though everything is "fine"? When we say, "Praise to you, Lord Jesus Christ," what's going on in our hearts? Are we disconnected, unmoved, or uncommitted? Are we actually saying, "Whatever, God. It's fine," to get him off our backs?

In your Holy Hour, you need to be brutally honest with Jesus. He wants an authentic relationship with you. If you are upset with Jesus, tell him that you're upset. If you're experiencing a broken heart, tell him. If you're being tempted toward a certain sin, lay it out for him. St. Ignatius of Loyola was a master of prayer and the spiritual life. He created a way of prayer called the Spiritual Exercises. An important part of this was St. Ignatius's emphasis on our inner life: our thoughts, feelings, and desires. We experience thoughts, feelings, and desires in our hearts when we pray. This is one of the ways that God communicates with us. Let's go through each of these inner movements:

Tell God Your Thoughts: In your Holy Hour, reflect on the thoughts that you are having. Write them down if you find it helpful. What is preoccupying your thoughts right now? What is taking up the biggest space in your mind? What is holding your attention?

Be honest with Jesus about what you are thinking. We can get distracted in prayer easily. We think about things that seem "less than holy." However, sometimes Jesus wants us to concentrate on the thoughts that are distracting us. If I'm in Holy Hour and I'm distracted by a crappy conversation I had, Jesus wants to know about it. He wants to redeem it! If I'm distracted by something I'm anxious about, Jesus wants to know about my anxieties. He wants me to be brutally honest with him so he can love me in those anxieties.

Share Your Feelings with God: St. Ignatius encouraged those practicing the Spiritual Exercises to pay attention to emotions during prayer. Who created our emotions? God! God uses our emotions to communicate himself. Jesus experienced all things except for sin. He experienced the emotions that we experience. Emotions aren't sinful . . . they come from our inner being.

During your Holy Hour, relate your emotions to Jesus.

Acknowledge Your Desires to God: The desires within our hearts motivate us. We have desires for things that are holy and things that are not holy. All authentic desires come from God, but sometimes the desires need to be purified.

One of our students here at the Newman Center shared with me recently a desire that she experienced in her prayer. She desired to date this certain boy and was brutally honest with Jesus about it. Because she wasn't ashamed of the desire, she brought it to the Lord and he began to gently purify her desire. She came to realize that her desire to date this boy wasn't the deepest part of her desire; it was to be "wanted." Jesus gently showed her that what she desired—to be "wanted"—was to be found in him. That desire to be loved and known is something God places in our hearts. When we give him our raw desires, the Lord begins to purify those desires, and his purification of our desires brings us closer and closer to him.

Three Approaches to Holy Hour Prayer

As Nacho Libre would say, "Let's get down to the nitty-gritty" of the Holy Hour! In the second section of the book, you'll have the awesome opportunity to experience three different methods of prayer after each daily reflection. These three approaches literally changed my life when I was in seminary. It took me until I was twenty-three years old to realize *God actually shows up* when I pray. My spiritual director taught me about these three approaches. They are easy and effective, not to mention . . . God shows up.

Lectio Divina

Lectio divina, or "divine reading," is an ancient form of praying with scripture. For centuries the Church has encouraged the faithful to read and meditate on scripture. Each day of our thirty days together, you will have an opportunity to practice lectio divina. Here is a step-by-step guide to the practice of lectio divina.

Lectio (Reading): Choose a scripture passage to meditate on; then read it through once, slowly, to grasp the story and the context. After reading it one time through, read it again, even more slowly, paying attention to any words or phrases that stand out to you. If nothing stands out, read it a third time and pay attention to your thoughts, feelings, and desires.

For example, I choose Matthew 14:22–33: Jesus walks on water. I read it through twice. When I read about Peter beginning to sink, the word *sink* stands out to me. So I write it down and ask God to show me the significance of that word.

Meditatio (Meditation): Meditatio is when you start to dive into the words that stand out to you. You ponder the words and the imagery of the passage. Bishop Robert Barron, in one of his YouTube videos about prayer, talks about praying "like a cow."[11] A cow chews on its food very intentionally and very slowly, sucking out every single bit of moisture from the food. In meditatio you are chewing slowly all of the beautiful words and images of the passage.

For example, I keep thinking of Peter sinking, and I start imagining what that looked like. I begin to imagine myself in the place of Peter, feeling helpless as I sink into the ocean.

Oratio (Pray/Speak): Oratio is the time to speak to the Lord. In oratio you are called to begin a dialogue with God. Think about what you were meditating on and what you wish to share with the Lord. It could be a few words or a whole discourse. Let the conversation with God flow naturally.

For example, "Jesus, I feel like I'm sinking with my studies. I feel like I can't breathe because I'm overwhelmed. Please help me like you helped St. Peter!"

Contemplatio (Contemplation): Contemplatio is nothing more than being with the Lord, resting in his presence. After sharing what is in your heart, you spend time with the Lord in silence. Have you ever noticed your grandparents or an older couple sit with each other without speaking? It's like that! They are in love with each other and so comfortable with each other that they can just "be." We do that with Jesus during contemplatio, and we wait to hear anything that the Lord may say to us.

For example, I make a habit of spending ten minutes with the Lord near the end of Holy Hour. In the silence I feel a greater and more profound peace. My heart feels tons of hope in God. I no longer feel as if I am sinking!

Lectio divina sounds complex, but it is very simple. As Christians, we are all called to enter into this beautiful form of prayer. Each day you'll have an opportunity to practice this, and you can come back to this page to refresh your knowledge of the steps.

Imaginative Prayer

Imaginative prayer is another form of prayer that you will practice each day during your thirty days. It is exactly how it sounds. We use our imagination in our prayer. If you are a daydreamer, had an imaginary friend growing up (or still do), or thought of creative games to play with your friends, this kind of prayer is for you! If you have trouble imagining things out of nothing or you don't consider yourself a creative, this kind of prayer is *also* for you!

The God of the Universe created you. He created your mind, and therefore he created your imagination. We can often think our imagination is this rogue element of our body that isn't connected to anything "holy." But God is so good that he created and delights in every aspect of your person—from your body to your soul and your mind.

During each of the thirty days, after the lectio divina portion, you will have an opportunity to practice imaginative prayer. I provide questions to help you engage your imagination and allow God to use your imagination to speak to your heart.

The most common roadblock to imaginative prayer is doubt. You might wonder, "Did I just make this up? How do I know this was God and not just my imagination?" Remember, Jesus gave you the gift of your imagination. During your Holy Hour, ask yourself if the imaginative prayer brought peace, joy, unity, and a desire for holiness. Those are the fruits that come from Jesus. If you experience confusion, division, fear, or doubt, those are the fruits of a bad spirit. Jesus is in the peace. He is not in the fear or division. Move toward the peace. Stay away from the fear!

Journaling

You will have the opportunity to journal in each of the thirty Holy Hours. There are spaces provided after each of the reflections or you can use your own journal if you have one. If you have never journaled or kept a diary before, it is simpler than you may think. Journaling is nothing more than recording your prayer. Countless spiritual masters from the Church journaled, including St. Ignatius of Loyola, St. Thérèse of Lisieux, Henri Nouwen, Thomas Merton, and St. Teresa of Avila.

Journaling is not only spiritually helpful but also psychologically helpful. Writing down thoughts and experiences by hand can help improve memory retention and recall. It helps with our mental health and improves our emotional regulation.[12] In her book *The Gifts of Imperfection,* the social science researcher Brené Brown emphasizes the importance of journaling. She stresses how journaling can lead to greater self-knowledge. She suggests that the more we journal, the more likely we are to pick up on negative self-talk and self-deprecation. Journaling frees us from anxiety and helps us to simply be kind to ourselves.

On the spiritual level, journaling helps us remember what God is doing in our hearts. As human beings we easily forget what happened just a week ago. Or we dismiss it, lying to ourselves that "it was all just a dream." Journaling reminds us of the God moments in the past that were "real." When we are having a dry period of prayer, previous journal entries can remind us of past real experiences with God. For example, on Wednesday I may make a Holy Hour and journal about how Jesus seems so close to me. The following Wednesday, if I'm having a bad day and my Holy Hour is dry, I can look back at the previous week and remember that what I experienced was *real.*

Since journaling doesn't come naturally to me, I've looked to other friends in my life to help with how best to journal. What impressed me is how unique journaling is to each person. One of my brother priests simply writes down the strongest thought, feeling, and desire that he experiences during his daily Holy Hour. A FOCUS missionary I know journals by writing a love letter to Jesus each Holy Hour. A religious sister shared with me that her journaling is simply telling Jesus about her day. You can also find guided journals, such as the *Living the Word Companion Journal* (to record your thoughts about scripture reading) or *The Ave Prayer Intentions Journal,* to guide you along the process.

If this is your first time journaling, start small. Write a few sentences, jotting down any graces from your prayer. After the first ten Holy Hours, look back on what you wrote. It is so awesome to see how God is *always* working in our hearts. The issue is, we easily forget . . .

As I mentioned before, these three approaches to prayer changed my life. I went from wondering if God actually listens to me to "Oh my lanta, God shows up when I pray!" Please, please, please practice lectio divina, imaginative prayer, and journaling each day of the challenge. Your life will be changed, too!

Lectio divina immerses you in God's literal Word. He reveals himself and his love for you in imaginative prayer. He speaks through you and reminds you of his presence in your journaling. Everything in part 2 is laid out for you. Read the reflection; then pray. Or better yet, read the reflection—then *live.*

MEETING JESUS WHERE I NEED HIM MOST

The 30 Days

Batman has Robin. Harry has Ron. Michael has Dwight. The Mandalorian has Grogu. Naruto has Sasuke. Sherlock has Watson. Each of these main characters needs their supporting character. Without their support, they become lost.

When it comes to our relationship with Jesus, we need the support of the Church. Jesus Christ, through the Church, gives us unlimited grace and support for our life of prayer. This next section lays out the support especially helpful in our thirty-day journey. Don't ignore free support! Embrace grace. Yes, Batman has Robin, but St. [*insert your name here*] has the Church.

Become Fully Alive!

In the fall of 2022, the student leaders (called the COR team) of the Newman Center where I am chaplain organized and prepped the fall retreat on campus and came up with the theme "The Abundant Life." They had noticed that so many students on campus were living like zombies, barely alive—phones out, eyes glazed, no passion or emotion. Most students were not finding their college years to be life-giving. We wanted them to find *abundant* life in Jesus, to experience what it means to be *fully alive.*

I was incredibly inspired by the deep desire in student leaders' hearts. The theme of being "fully alive" with Jesus remained in my own heart as I began to notice so many young people dragging themselves through life without joy, peace, or fulfillment. All of us have experienced this lack of fulfillment—maybe you are right now. So, if you desire *more*, keep reading and be prepared for an outpouring of Christ's life!

Jesus Christ promised us life: "A thief comes only to steal and slaughter and destroy; I came so that they might have life and have it more abundantly" (Jn 10:10). Jesus Christ *is* the abundant life. If you were to visit our Newman Center or any Newman Center throughout the country, the students who have a consistent and intentional prayer life with Jesus are the most alive!

The closer we get to Jesus Christ, the more alive we become. My prayer for you is that by engaging these thirty reflections and spending quality time with Jesus, each Holy Hour will draw you more and more into that abundant life he wants for you. You are in my thoughts and prayers as you enter into a deeper relationship with Jesus. Reject the zombie life. Embrace the abundant life!

How? Glad you asked . . . keep reading.

Establish a Holy Hour "Habit"

Vladimir Horowitz is considered one of the greatest pianists of the twentieth century. To this day, composers and pianists look up to Horowitz for his incredible technical skill and passion. When asked how often he practiced to keep up with his technical skills, he answered, "If I skip practice for one day, I notice. If I skip practice for two days, my wife notices. If I skip for three days, the world notices."[1]

Horowitz's words of wisdom totally relate to our commitment to a regular Holy Hour—whether your goal is a couple of times a week on a set day and time or thirty days in a row as you read through this book. Whatever you decide, it's important to make a commitment and stick with it.

Why is that commitment so important? Any time we try to establish a new healthy practice, it's too easy to slip back into old habits unless we exercise a little fortitude. For example, imagine you are establishing a healthy eating pattern. If you binge on donuts or buffalo wings on your cheat day, it's no big deal; you can follow up with healthy foods the following day. But if you have two cheat days in a row, it's a dangerous slippery slope.

It's the same way with spiritual habits like a regular Holy Hour. If we miss once, it's a mistake that we can easily recover from. If we miss twice, it's harder to get back into the routine. If we miss three times, the habit never sticks—we just go back to our old ways.

When it comes to our relationship with Jesus, consistency matters. Thirty minutes a day with the King of the Universe is far more fruitful and life-giving than spending a few hours in church on Sunday and then ghosting him for the rest of the week. Not just for the next thirty days but in general, we are free to make mistakes and to fail, but we can't make mistakes a habit. Jesus makes himself totally available to us. We have everything we need to have a divine friendship with him. Here are three other important ways you can supercharge your soul and build up your relationship with Jesus.

Go to Daily Mass

If you are "spiritual strength training" over these next thirty days as you establish your Holy Hour habit, consider going to daily Mass. Sunday Mass, of course, is nonnegotiable. Daily Mass, though, is highly encouraged for these thirty days.

The Second Vatican Council stressed that the Eucharist is the "source and summit" of our faith. Everything flows into and back out of the Mass. Part of me feels we should just scrap the thirty days of Holy Hours and just go to Mass for thirty days. However, the thirty days are about developing a habit of intentional prayer with Jesus, so going to daily Mass can enhance and supercharge your Holy Hour, especially if you make your Holy Hour right before or after Mass. Imagine receiving Jesus Christ in the Eucharist and then spending a Holy Hour savoring his presence within you. It's like the greatest, most life-giving backstage pass ever!

Hit the Confessional

What is better than being free? On a daily basis, so many things weigh us down, and we become slaves to our thoughts, addictions, and temptations. There is a deep desire in our hearts for freedom. The Sacrament of Confession is our full-access pass to freedom. Jesus frees us from whatever sins enslave us. He wins in our hearts every single time we go to Confession.

Confession is highly encouraged at least once during these thirty days. I would recommend going sometime after day 20. The first twenty days concentrate on interior and exterior influences that plague our lives. There will most likely be things that will resonate in your heart you'll wish to bring to Jesus in Confession.

Find a Spiritual Director

Jesus never wants us to go it alone. We need big brothers and big sisters in the faith who can help us to see where Jesus is in our lives. The walk to Emmaus is a great example of this. In the Gospel of Luke, two disciples are walking along the road from Jerusalem to the town of Emmaus. The disciples are recounting and trying to understand everything that happened to

Jesus. Suddenly a man begins walking along the road with them and revealing to them who God is through the scriptures. By the end of their journey together, they recognize that the man is Jesus.

Spiritual direction is very similar: two disciples walking along the way together, identifying where Jesus is. A spiritual director can help identify where Jesus is in your prayer. Sometimes we are so caught up in our own thoughts and emotions that we lose track of where Jesus is and what he is doing in our hearts.

Spiritual direction isn't required but highly encouraged. If you know a priest, religious sister, or trained campus minister that you feel comfortable around, feel free to ask them to meet once or twice during these thirty days to help you process what you've been experiencing in your Holy Hours. Again, Jesus never wants you to go it alone. We are all the Body of Christ, helping to build each other up to be future saints.

Follow ASTAR: How to Structure Your Holy Hour

Below is my suggestion for how to structure your Holy Hour, especially if you're new to this practice. Feel free to modify the structure any way you want. The goal is to experience deeper intimacy with Christ.

For example, if you spend an entire hour and never get past step 3, praise God . . . you must have gotten lost in your heart-to-heart with God! Some prayer forms may resonate more with you than others: you may experience total white noise when you're going through lectio divina but find the imaginative prayer is abundantly fruitful. Don't try to force yourself to go back to lectio. Stay with the imaginative prayer. Remain where the grace is!

However you decide to structure your time, here are five steps you can follow as the Holy Spirit guides you. If it helps, remember the Magi and follow ASTAR:

- **A**pproach: Enter into the Holy Hour recognizing you are in God's presence.
- **S**ilence: Take a few moments to focus and to brush aside any distractions.
- **T**alk: Tell Jesus what is on your heart, boldly and honestly.
- **A**ttend: Read the reflection and "chew" on it with lectio divina, imaginative prayer, and journaling.
- **R**eceive: Sit back and listen to what Jesus wants to say to you.

Let's break these down, one at a time.

Approach: The easiest step: we show up! We approach the Lord who is always waiting for us. At the beginning of your Holy Hour, take a few minutes to recognize you are in God's presence. God is present. He is with you! This process is like turning on a light in a dark room. Sometimes in prayer, it's as if we are just sitting in a dark room and talking to someone who *might be there.* We need to welcome the Holy Spirit and ask him to "turn on the light," so we can recognize he is there. Approach the Lord of the Universe and just show up! He is waiting.

Silence: It can be tempting to rush in and go directly into "word vomit" mode, pouring everything out to the Lord. Instead, take a few minutes of silence to just *be* with him. Silence can magnify the emotions that are on our hearts. Allow the silence to help you identify what you are truly feeling. Look back at page 12 to identify your thoughts, feelings, and desires.

Talk: Share your heart with Jesus. Relate to him your thoughts, feelings, and desires. Tell him about your day. Look back at page 13. Be brutally honest with him.

Attend: Focus your attention on the reflection for the day. Follow with each of the prayer exercises, starting with lectio divina (see page 16), then imaginative prayer (page 17), and finally journaling (page 18) about anything that struck your heart or any graces you received from Jesus.

Receive: This is your time to rest with Jesus and receive from him. Listen to what he wants to say to you. Allow him to love you. You don't have to do or accomplish anything. You get to be loved as a beloved son or daughter.

Okay, now that you have the structure and tools you need to get started, let's begin our challenge—one Holy Hour at a time!

JESUS, I NEED YOU.
PLEASE HELP ME.

The First 10 Days

We are our own worst enemies. The lies that we tell ourselves, the negative thoughts that we dwell on, and the harsh accusations plague our interior thoughts and prevent us from being fully alive in Jesus. The first ten days will address the inside. Our interior thoughts and feelings can prevent us from living life to the fullest.

St. Thomas Aquinas said that if you want to make progress in the spiritual life, you must first attend to the interior life.[1] Be gentle with yourself and your interior thoughts and feelings that may come up during this section. Remember that Jesus is gentle with us and never accuses. He is promising you abundant life!

Day 1

FEELING UNSEEN?

Jesus Sees Me

It is Jesus that you seek when you dream of happiness; he is waiting for you when nothing else satisfies.

—St. John Paul the Great

As a college chaplain, I hear an abundance of heartbreaking stories that reveal a need for God. One story in particular has stuck with me, and I want to share it here because I think it is relatable to all of us, especially as we begin these thirty days.

Over the past few years, I've gotten to know Amy (not her real name), a college student who recently experienced a breakup with her boyfriend. She had been dating him for a significant amount of time, and she was not expecting what happened. It was totally out of the blue. Now, it's difficult enough to break up with a significant other when the writing is on the wall, but to have it come out of nowhere hurts!

Directly after the breakup, Amy was shocked, wounded, angry, depressed, and misunderstood. For months she experienced feelings of unworthiness and confusion, which led to a lack of hope. Then as Amy began to come to terms with what was happening, she saw her former boyfriend for the first time at a college football game. In the midst of the crowd walking to and from the bleachers, Amy saw her ex walking directly toward her. They glanced at each other briefly, and as they passed each other it was obvious to Amy that he didn't even recognize her.

She felt completely invisible. Shocked and hurt, she lost her footing, tripped, and fell against the bleacher wall. She felt as if she were face down in the dirt, surrounded by strangers, and totally unseen.

When Amy first told me this story, it wrecked me. Amy has a dynamite personality, and everyone who knows her loves being around her. It's not fair that Amy should struggle with a fear of not being "seen" or feeling unworthy or unvalued. However, hers is not a unique struggle in our culture. So many of us feel unseen at some point. We ask ourselves, "Will I always be alone? Am I just destined to be anonymous?"

Praise God, that is not the end of Amy's story. She shared with me that at her lowest moment, as she knelt there in the dirt, "the person who I wanted to see me (my ex) . . . didn't. But in that moment I thought of someone I had lost sight of, someone I had forgotten about and ignored. Until that moment, I was too blind to see him (Jesus). But when I did . . . it was the beginning of my realignment with God."

In the moments when no one else saw her, Jesus Christ saw her. That experience is painted throughout the gospels. The blind, the lame, prostitutes, beggars, and tax collectors all were put at a distance from the culture. They were unseen. But Jesus Christ entered into our world to "see" and "know" them. At your lowest, at your most vulnerable, *you are seen*. During these thirty days, *you are seen and you are not alone*. Jesus Christ is walking with you every day, seeing you, and you will never be the same.

LECTIO DIVINA

John 20:11–18

But Mary stayed outside the tomb weeping. And as she wept, she bent over into the tomb and saw two angels in white sitting there, one at the head and one at the feet where the body of

Jesus had been. And they said to her, "Woman, why are you weeping?" She said to them, "They have taken my Lord, and I don't know where they laid him." When she had said this, she turned around and saw Jesus there, but did not know it was Jesus. Jesus said to her, "Woman, why are you weeping? Whom are you looking for?" She thought it was the gardener and said to him, "Sir, if you carried him away, tell me where you laid him, and I will take him." Jesus said to her, "Mary!" She turned and said to him in Hebrew, "Rabbouni," which means Teacher. Jesus said to her, "Stop holding on to me, for I have not yet ascended to the Father. But go to my brothers and tell them, 'I am going to my Father and your Father, to my God and your God.'" Mary of Magdala went and announced to the disciples, "I have seen the Lord," and what he told her.

IMAGINATIVE PRAYER

When I was a newly minted first-year seminarian, Cardinal Francis George visited Mundelein Seminary to give a talk and to spend time with all the Chicago seminarians. Everyone knew Cardinal George (obviously, he was a cardinal . . .). He wrote amazing books and preached inspiring homilies. I had never met him but had always wanted to.

After the talk, I was walking back to my room and I saw Cardinal George in the hall, walking toward me (very similar to Amy and her ex). I got very nervous and was awkwardly trying to figure out what to say. Before I could say anything, the cardinal looked at me and very casually said, "Ah, Tim, have a good night!"

I was speechless. My first thought was, "Oh my gosh, he knows me!" My second thought was, "Oh my gosh, I feel great!" When we are seen and known, it enlivens us to give more of ourselves in gratitude and love.

In your prayer, imagine being in a situation where you have felt unseen. Imagine Jesus there in that situation with you, and *he sees you and says your name.*

JOURNALING

Use the space below to journal about your Holy Hour.

Day 2

JUDGED?

Jesus Knows and Loves Me

God loves each of us as if there were only one of us.
—St. Augustine of Hippo

If being unseen and unknown is a problem, so is the opposite extreme—to be exposed and vulnerable to the entire world. Condemned harshly, without mercy. In other words, to be judged.

Sometimes we do it ourselves. Our judgy voices blare in our heads as we scroll through someone's social media feed. You can almost hear the voices coming out of the darkness: "Oh, I know you. I know everything about you. I know the real you."

People can so easily find out everything about us, for good or for bad. Yet that knowledge is so often not tempered with love. To be known and not loved is a recipe for objectification, anxiety, and resentment. Just imagine if your entire life was on Instagram and everyone could watch the *reels* of your life story, including the most shameful parts of your life. Imagine everyone knowing everything about you but from a distance without any love.

The Gospel of John describes Jesus's encounter with a woman caught in adultery. The woman is brought in front of the crowd in the Temple area. Everyone sees her and knows her shame. You can almost hear the accusing whispers: "Oh, I know you. I know everything about you. I know the real you." The woman is known but not loved. Her shame is exposed.

Then Jesus encounters the woman, sees her, and at a glance knows everything about her. The significant difference is that he *loves* her. Jesus sees her shame, and he receives her with a gentle but life-changing love. He then calls her to "go, [and] from now on do not sin any more" (Jn 8:11).

If you want to grow in your relationship with Jesus, and if you want to diffuse the shame in your heart, give Jesus permission to know your shame and love you in your shame. Then allow the Lord to call you to virtue, to build you up to *go and sin no more.*

LECTIO DIVINA

John 8:1–11

Then each went to his own house, while Jesus went to the Mount of Olives. But early in the morning he arrived again in the temple area, and all the people started coming to him, and he sat down and taught them. Then the scribes and the Pharisees brought a woman who had been caught in adultery and made her stand in the middle. They said to him, "Teacher, this woman was caught in the very act of committing adultery. Now in the law, Moses commanded us to stone such women. So what do you say?" They said this to test him, so that they could have some charge to bring against him. Jesus bent down and began to write on the ground with his finger. But when they continued asking him, he straightened up and said to them, "Let the one among you who is without sin be the first to throw a stone at her." Again he bent down and wrote on the ground. And in response, they went away one by one, beginning with the elders. So he was left alone with the woman before him. Then Jesus straightened up and said to her, "Woman, where are they? Has no one condemned you?" She replied, "No one, sir." Then Jesus said, "Neither do I condemn you. Go, [and] from now on do not sin any more."

IMAGINATIVE PRAYER

Think of times in your life when you were known but not loved. Imagine Jesus entering into those moments. Gently he reminds you that he knows and loves you. What does it feel like to be known and loved?

JOURNALING

Use the space below to journal about your Holy Hour.

Day 3

UNWORTHY?

Jesus Created the Good in Me

It's not our own works that make us worthy but the
grace of Christ who lives in us.

—**St. Gregory of Nyssa**

Of all the superhero movies, my absolute favorite is the first
Captain America. Set during World War II, the main character, Steve Rogers, wants to go and fight for his country. The
problem is that Rogers is kind of *puny*. Very small and not at
all muscular, he does not have qualities that the military is
looking for. Yet despite his weakness, Rogers is a *good man*. He
is incredibly brave and has a great heart. Bottom line: Rogers
is weak but very, very good.

Among all the candidates to try the "super soldier serum,"
Steve Rogers is the most unlikely. All the other candidates are
tall, muscular, perfect military specimens. But the doctor in
charge of the super soldier serum recognizes that all the candidates lack *heart* and *goodness*. When Rogers is chosen to receive
the serum, he asks the doctor, "Why me?" He tells Rogers,

> The serum amplifies everything that is inside. So, good
> becomes great. Bad becomes worse. This is why you were
> chosen. Because a strong man, who has known power all
> his life, will lose respect for that power. But a weak man
> knows the value of strength, and knows compassion.[2]

Rogers receives the serum and becomes Captain America.
His "goodness" is magnified and he becomes great! This is the

Good News that Jesus Christ has for us. From the beginning of time, the God of the Universe created man and woman, and they were *good*. Man and woman were made in God's image and likeness. You were created good. You are made in his image and likeness. You are absolutely worthy!

Before the serum, Steve Rogers was very good but weak. Similarly, we are also very good but weak. In our weakness we are led to temptation and sin. When we sin, we feel as if we are unworthy of Jesus's love. This leads to self-doubt and a lack of self-worth. Jesus Christ is reminding you right now that you were created good, and you are always worthy of his love. We have to continue to turn back to him and receive the super soldier serum, which is his grace. And his grace transforms us from good to great, from great to *saints*.

LECTIO DIVINA

Genesis 1:26–31

Then God said: Let us make human beings in our image, after our likeness. Let them have dominion over the fish of the sea, the birds of the air, the tame animals, all the wild animals, and all the creatures that crawl on the earth.

> God created mankind in his image;
>> in the image of God he created them;
>> male and female he created them.

God blessed them and God said to them: Be fertile and multiply; fill the earth and subdue it. Have dominion over the fish of the sea, the birds of the air, and all the living things that crawl on the earth. God also said: See, I give you every seed-bearing plant on all the earth and every tree that has seed-bearing fruit on it to be your food; and to all the wild animals, all the birds of the air, and all the living creatures that crawl on the earth, I give all the green plants for food. And so it happened. God looked at everything he had made and found it very good. Evening came, and morning followed—the sixth day.

IMAGINATIVE PRAYER

Imagine how Jesus was looking at you when you were born. Imagine how he looked at you when your parents baptized you. Imagine how he looks at you right now. He created you good. You are worthy. How does Jesus look at his good and worthy creation?

JOURNALING

Use the space below to journal about your Holy Hour.

Day 4

ANXIOUS?

Jesus Gives Me Peace

Pray, hope, and don't worry. Anxiety doesn't help at all. Our merciful Lord will listen to your prayer.

—St. Pio of Pietrelcina

This past December I had the incredible privilege of giving a talk to fifteen hundred high schoolers from around the Diocese of Venice, Florida. It was the largest group of teens I'd ever spoken to, and before the talk, I experienced heightened anxiety. As I began the talk, my heart was pumping out of my chest and my hands were sweaty.

Shortly into the talk, I told the teens, "Raise your hand if you've ever struggled with anxiety." All fifteen hundred teens raised their hands! After that moment, my anxiety was diffused. Clearly I was not alone in the struggle. This boosted my confidence in speaking, and I felt free to do what God wanted me to do, which was to proclaim *him* to the teens. What increased my confidence was simply knowing that I was not alone.

You are not alone either.

Anxiety is everywhere. I witness it on my college campus every single day. It permeates all cultures, all ages, and all occupations. Anxiety even plagues people whom you wouldn't expect: Adele, Ryan Reynolds, Emma Stone, Stephen Colbert, and Michael Phelps are just a few people who have spoken honestly and publicly about their experience of anxiety. How about you? Do you ever share your anxieties aloud so they lose their power over you?

This thirty-day journey is moving you toward being *fully alive*. Anxiety prevents us from being fully alive. We become slaves to *worry* and forget to allow Jesus into the present moment. Anxiety makes us ask, "What if . . . ?"

- What if I didn't study enough for the exam?
- What if I never get married?
- What if he doesn't ask me to prom?
- What if God wants me to do something I don't want to do?
- What if I'm not accepted?

All of these "what ifs" are about the future. They're never about the present. My experience of anxiety with the fifteen hundred teens certainly fell in that category: "What if I suck? What if the teens can't relate to me? What if I faint on the stage?" However, in the present moment, the anxiety faded away once I knew I was safe.

In 2020, the most-read and most-bookmarked passage in the Bible was Isaiah 41:10: "Do not fear: I am with you; do not be anxious: I am your God. I will strengthen you, I will help you, I will uphold you with my victorious right hand." God is the ultimate answer to our struggle with anxiety. He reminds us time and time again through scripture that we can trust him.

The famous Catholic speaker and writer Jason Evert came to Chicago when I was in college. I remember listening to him talk about St. John Paul II's smile. St. John Paul II had a smile that communicated *I know who wins* . . . Jesus Christ is obviously the one who wins. He is the ultimate diffuser of all anxiety.

Jesus promised us peace and promised himself, and he proved it in his Paschal Mystery. I encourage you to use Google Images to search for St. John Paul II's smile. This is the same man who was persecuted by communists in Poland and shot by an assassin in St. Peter's Square in Rome. Nothing shook him from his obvious joy in Jesus Christ because he was utterly convicted that Love himself would always win.

During this Holy Hour, allow Jesus to remind you that he has won, is winning, and will win in your life. Give him your anxieties throughout these thirty days, and let Jesus be the great diffuser of your anxiety.

LECTIO DIVINA

Philippians 4:4–7

Rejoice in the Lord always. I shall say it again: rejoice! Your kindness should be known to all. The Lord is near. Have no anxiety at all, but in everything, by prayer and petition, with thanksgiving, make your requests known to God. Then the peace of God that surpasses all understanding will guard your hearts and minds in Christ Jesus.

IMAGINATIVE PRAYER

Today's lectio scripture is written by St. Paul to the church in Philippi. He wrote this letter from a prison in Rome, proclaiming joy and rejecting anxiety from a prison cell! Anxiety can be such a prison, preventing us from being fully alive. Imagine your greatest anxieties and bring them to Jesus during this Holy Hour. Be honest with him and ask him to diffuse these anxieties. Imagine how he acts toward you. Imagine what he says to you.

JOURNALING

Use the space below to journal about your Holy Hour.

Day 5
RESTLESS?
Jesus Makes Me Content

You have made us for yourself, O Lord, and our
hearts are restless until they rest in you.

—St. Augustine of Hippo

Four years ago, I was giving a talk to the teens at my parish assignment. Taking a poll, I asked the teens a question: "Besides Jesus, obviously, who in the world at the present moment is the GOAT (Greatest of All Time)?" I received several shouts of "Michael Jordan!" and "Michael Phelps!" A few "Serena Williams" and one sad, lonely "Bruce Willis." But the vast majority shouted out "Tom Brady!" I found it fascinating how so many teens looked up to this quarterback and all his accomplishments: 251 games won, 23 NFL seasons, 7,753 completions, five-time Super Bowl MVP, and seven-time Super Bowl champion. No matter if you disagree with his GOAT-ness, Brady is incredibly accomplished.

On a 2005 episode of *60 Minutes*, Tom Brady was asked what it's like to win three Super Bowls. What he said blew my mind: "Why do I have three Super Bowl rings and still think there's something greater out there for me? I mean, maybe a lot of people would say, 'Hey man, this is what is.' I reached my goal, my dream, my life. Me, I think, 'God, it's gotta be more than this. I mean, this can't be what it's all cracked up to be . . .'"[3]

Tom Brady restless? Unsure of his identity? When he has literally *everything*? Even among the GOATS, and among

47

heaven's GOATS (the saints), there is always a restlessness that is never satisfied. That little restlessness can only be filled by Jesus Christ. He is our rest. He is our fulfillment!

During my senior year of college, studying linguistics, I was offered a chance to go to Quantico and start a career with the FBI. At the same time, I was dating an incredible woman who was everything I desired in a future wife. I was close to my family and had an intimate circle of friends. From the outside, I felt like Tom Brady, having everything I could ever want. Yet interiorly I was empty. I experienced restlessness every day. Everything felt vain.

All the exterior successes weren't satisfying. I already knew that this restlessness and emptiness could only be filled by Jesus. The world was saying, "This is everything you could ever want! A career with the FBI! An awesome girlfriend! Solid circle of friends!" But Jesus was speaking gently into my heart, reminding me that he was my fulfillment. Soon after all this took place during my senior year, I entered into seminary to fill the emptiness with Jesus. I have never felt that emptiness since.

St. Augustine famously said to Jesus, "You have made us for yourself, O Lord, and our hearts are restless until they rest in You."[4] Right now, are you restless? Are you searching? Are you feeling that nothing is filling the emptiness of your heart? Jesus Christ is your fulfillment.

LECTIO DIVINA

Matthew 19:23–30

Then Jesus said to his disciples, "Amen, I say to you, it will be hard for one who is rich to enter the kingdom of heaven. Again I say to you, it is easier for a camel to pass through the eye of a needle than for one who is rich to enter the kingdom of God." When the disciples heard this, they were greatly astonished and said, "Who then can be saved?" Jesus looked at them and said, "For human beings this is impossible, but for God all things are possible." Then Peter said to him in reply, "We have given up everything and followed you. What will there be for us?" Jesus said to them, "Amen, I say to you that you who have followed me, in the new age, when the Son of Man is seated on his throne of glory, will yourselves sit on twelve thrones, judging the twelve tribes of Israel. And everyone who has given up houses or brothers or sisters or father or mother or children or lands for the sake of my name will receive a hundred times more, and will inherit eternal life. But many who are first will be last, and the last will be first.

IMAGINATIVE PRAYER

Imagine having the things that you want most in life. What are those things? Be specific: amazing spouse, perfect job, dream home, best-friend group, and so forth. Will that be enough to satisfy the restlessness that you experience? If you have everything you want here on earth, do you really need heaven? Do you really need Jesus?

Now imagine those things slowly slipping through your fingers: Circumstances change. Wealth and health fluctuate. People die. Nothing is guaranteed . . . except Jesus. What places in your heart will never be satisfied by anything from this world?

JOURNALING

Use the space below to journal about your Holy Hour.

Day 6

INSECURE?

I'm Made in God's Image

Jesus alone is the perfect model of virtue, and He
alone can teach us to love.

—St. Thérèse of Lisieux

My little brother and I have been on a magical journey of
watching the entire collection of Dwayne "The Rock" John-
son's movies. One of the first movies that we watched was
Jumanji: Welcome to the Jungle. Remember the start of the
movie, when the high school girl who is later transformed
into Jack Black's character is taking a selfie on her couch for
her social media? The scene shows her struggling to move into
the perfect position to get the selfie. She's holding a selfie stick
while moving her coffee mug into the frame and frantically
trying to get her hair flowing correctly. Sounds like reality,
right?

So many of us struggle with insecurities about our personality or body image because everything we see on social media
is perfect! In 2017, the same year *Jumanji* was released, the
Royal Society for Public Health cautioned parents about the
negative effects of social media platforms such as Instagram,
Snapchat, and Facebook on young people's mental health.
They found through their survey that these platforms were
contributing to anxiety, depression, poor body image, and
low self-esteem.[5] Frequent social media use can also lead to an
increase in appearance-focused behaviors, such as comparing
oneself to others and seeking validation through likes and

comments, which can contribute to body dissatisfaction and lower self-esteem.[6]

As my high school freshman religion teacher would always say to us, "Comparing leads to despairing!" Nothing good comes from comparing ourselves to others. God created you to be secure in how he created you. You are so good and worthy of love.

In her famous autobiography, *Story of a Soul*, St. Thérèse of Lisieux wrote about the dangers of comparison and insecurity. Thérèse was a young Carmelite nun who spent nine years of her life in the monastery until she died from tuberculosis at the age of twenty-four. In the introduction to the book, her superior, Mother Prioress, recounted the words of two of her sisters, who were talking about little Thérèse as she lay dying. She recounted, "I heard them say: 'What can we put in her obituary? She has done nothing.'"[7]

Thérèse was so secure in her identity that she never compared herself to others. She was only concerned about how Jesus Christ saw her! Imagine if we had that security in our identity. Am I more concerned with how other people see me or how Jesus sees me? St. Thérèse of Lisieux is a saint for many reasons, but what stands out to me is how she rooted her identity and security in Jesus.

Comparing leads to despairing; letting Jesus be our security leads to freedom!

LECTIO DIVINA

Matthew 8:23–27

He got into a boat and his disciples followed him. Suddenly a violent storm came up on the sea, so that the boat was being swamped by waves; but he was asleep. They came and woke him, saying, "Lord, save us! We are perishing!" He said to them, "Why are you terrified, O you of little faith?" Then he got up, rebuked the winds and the sea, and there was great calm. The men were amazed and said, "What sort of man is this, whom even the winds and the sea obey?"

IMAGINATIVE PRAYER

Imagine yourself with God the Father. What does the Father look like to you? How does the Father make you feel secure? Do you feel like you need to compare yourself to others when you are with God the Father?

JOURNALING

Use the space below to journal about your Holy Hour.

Day 7

OVERWHELMED?

I Am Present with Jesus

> The present moment is the only moment in which
> we can touch God. Let us make the most of it.
>
> **—St. Teresa of Avila**

Congratulations—you've made it to day 7! I hope and pray you are slowly growing in your relationship with Jesus and becoming fully alive in him. This is the overall goal, of course—to be *fully alive* with Jesus.

So far we've talked about many of the roadblocks that get in the way of being fully alive: the lies that sneak into our hearts and make us feel unseen, judged, anxious, restless, and insecure. But one major roadblock that can affect every aspect of our health and spiritual life is the experience of being overwhelmed.

At our Newman Center, we have a coffee shop where some of our students learn how to be baristas. And they make such incredible coffee and latte art. As they take orders, grind the beans, and froth the milk, their primary concern is to stay in the present moment with the person they are serving. Jesus is present there. Evangelization is happening! The student baristas embrace the present moment with Jesus, and that leads to friendships, deep conversations, and authentic love.

This little oasis of intentionality is a stark contrast to what is going on in much of the rest of the college campus. It seems as if everyone who walks into the Newman Center is overwhelmed on some level, an experience that leads to deeper stress and anxiety and a sense of feeling out of control. In the spiritual life, feeling overwhelmed takes us out of the present moment and unable to be fully present to Jesus. We either experience tunnel vision about what needs to get done or become paralyzed and don't know what to do!

A while back, one of my priest brothers shared an awesome book with me: *The Martian* by Andy Weir. This recently became a movie starring Matt Damon, but I read the book before it was cool. The main character, Mark Watney, gets stranded on Mars, alone. He faces a series of challenges and obstacles on Mars in order to survive. If anyone in the world (or universe) should be feeling overwhelmed, it should be Watney. In the movie, Watney says something that's always resonated with me as he fought for his life:

> It's space. It's filled with chance, circumstance, and bad luck. It doesn't cooperate. At some point, I promise, at some point every single thing is gonna go south on you, and you'll think: this is it. This is how I end. And you can either accept that . . . or you can get to work. That's all it is. You simply begin. Solve one problem. Then the next one, then the next. You solve enough problems . . . and you get to come home.[8]

Watney focused on what he could control and worked diligently to solve each problem, one at a time. He focused on the present moment and what needed to get done. This approach of course can help us in our daily tasks and productivity skills. But on a spiritual level, when we are able to focus on the present moment, we get to experience what Jesus desires for us in that moment. Jesus Christ is living and real and true. He is not waiting for us in the future. We only have right now to be with him. In this very moment he is with you as you read this, and this is obviously where he wants you to be right now.

Be fully alive in Christ! Stay in the present moment with the Lord! That is the only sure antidote to feeling overwhelmed.

LECTIO DIVINA

Matthew 4:18–22

As he was walking by the Sea of Galilee, he saw two brothers, Simon who is called Peter, and his brother Andrew, casting a net into the sea; they were fishermen. He said to them, "Come after me, and I will make you fishers of men." At once they left their nets and followed him. He walked along from there and saw two other brothers, James, the son of Zebedee, and his brother John. They were in a boat, with their father Zebedee, mending their nets. He called them, and immediately they left their boat and their father and followed him.

IMAGINATIVE PRAYER

Imagine being with the apostles Peter and Andrew. How did they act in the present moment with Jesus by the Sea of Galilee? Imagine yourself as one of the apostles. How would you react? Would you be in the present moment? Would you be worried about the future? What does Jesus say to you? How do you react?

JOURNALING

Use the space below to journal about your Holy Hour.

Day 8

UNMOTIVATED?

I Will Stay and Wait on the Lord

Acedia is a sadness that is harmful to the soul
because it makes us reject every good that comes
from God.

—St. Thomas Aquinas

Do you ever feel a lack of motivation to pray? Is it incredibly
hard to even *want* to pay attention at Mass? Does a feeling
of boredom and tiredness kick in anytime you think about
engaging yourself in anything spiritual, as if you are in some
kind of spiritual rut?

Well, if you said yes to any of these questions, then congratulations—you're a human being! This specific vice that
was mentioned above in St. Thomas Aquinas's quote is called
acedia. Acedia is a resistance to anything holy. It is a spiritual
laziness. We all have days where we experience a tiredness
and it is difficult to enter into prayer. Acedia goes deeper than
just tiredness. It is a resistance to all spiritual things that will
help us to grow.

Imagine a couple, Anthony and Lauren, who have a pretty
solid dating relationship with each other. They obviously love
each other and care for each other's well-being. They have great
communication skills and are always willing to serve each
other. One day Anthony and Lauren get into a heated fight,
and after fighting Anthony walks away and Lauren calls off
the date early. They both go back to their apartments, sulk-
ing. The next day, instead of reaching out to each other to

59

fix things, they just ignore the situation—and each other. No calls, no texts, no contact. They begin to alienate each other because it's easier and doesn't take effort. Rather than engage in the conflict so that healing, forgiveness, and reconciliation can happen, Anthony and Lauren resist growth and change.

Believe it or not, this kind of resistance to change and growth can happen to any of us. Sometimes we would rather zone out at Mass than make the effort to hear what God has to say. When the Holy Spirit nudges us to grow in holiness and virtue, acedia whispers to us, "Nah . . . settle for less . . . just avoid . . . just escape."

I had the awesome opportunity to stay with a group of Benedictine monks in England on a retreat. During the retreat, I was struggling. Everything was a chore. I just didn't want to do all the things I was supposed to be doing. I avoided the chapel, and I escaped by going for runs and hikes. After I shared this experience of acedia with one of the monks, he told me, "Stay put." (And it was in an English accent, so it sounded even more profound.)

He told me that St. Benedict taught monks to "stay put" when they were experiencing a desire to escape. We are supposed to keep doing what we are supposed to be doing and wait for the Lord. He referred me to Psalm 27:14, "Wait for the Lord, take courage; be stouthearted, wait for the LORD!" When we experience acedia, don't try to escape and ignore the Holy Spirit's call to reconciliation. Just stay put and wait for the Lord!

LECTIO DIVINA

Matthew 26:36–45

Then Jesus came with them to a place called Gethsemane, and he said to his disciples, "Sit here while I go over there and pray." He took along Peter and the two sons of Zebedee, and began to feel sorrow and distress. Then he said to them, "My soul is sorrowful even to death. Remain here and keep watch with me." He advanced a little and fell prostrate in prayer, saying, "My Father, if it is possible, let this cup pass from me; yet, not as I will, but as you will." When he returned to his disciples he found them asleep. He said to Peter, "So you could not keep watch with me for one hour? Watch and pray that you may not undergo the test. The spirit is willing, but the flesh is weak." Withdrawing a second time, he prayed again, "My Father, if it is not possible that this cup pass without my drinking it, your will be done!" Then he returned once more and found them asleep, for they could not keep their eyes open. He left them and withdrew again and prayed a third time, saying the same thing again. Then he returned to his disciples and said to them, "Are you still sleeping and taking your rest? Behold, the hour is at hand when the Son of Man is to be handed over to sinners."

IMAGINATIVE PRAYER

Where has acedia crept into your life? What is your favorite method of escaping from Jesus? Imagine yourself staying put with Jesus. How do you feel staying put with him? Can you share with Jesus how you choose to escape from him?

JOURNALING

Use the space below to journal about your Holy Hour.

Day 9

ENVIOUS?

Let Jesus Un-Grinch My Heart

Envy is ever joined to the comparing of man's self;
and where there is no comparison, no envy.

—**Francis Bacon**

Before I was *Father* Tim, I was *Deacon* Tim. As a deacon in
seminary, I practiced a lot of preaching and public speaking.
I was always sad after we finished a practice session because I
was continuously comparing myself to the other deacons who
I thought were better than me. This made me feel sad, angry,
and full of self-doubt. The Church calls what I experienced
envy.

In the *Summa Theologica*, St. Thomas Aquinas describes
envy as a "sadness or sorrow at the good fortune of others."[9]
This is different from jealousy because jealousy is about want-
ing a *thing* that someone else has. For example, I'm jealous of
the new PlayStation 5 that my priest-buddy just got as a gift.
(Yes, priests play video games . . .) Envy, on the other hand, is
when we are sad, angry, or resentful when a person is *blessed*.
When I watched my brother seminarians give amazing homilies, I was sad because they were gifted. I was resentful because
they were blessed in their ability to give great homilies.

Have you ever been sad when someone is blessed in some
way? Have you ever felt resentment at a friend's gifts or talents?

St. Thomas Aquinas explains that the root of envy is *pride*.
Pride within our hearts causes us to think, "I deserve this gift,
too . . . I'm entitled to this, too . . . I deserve better . . ." This

exactly describes the discontentment that was in my heart in seminary: "I should be this talented . . . I am not satisfied with the gifts God gave me."

The antidote to this envy is gratitude and praise. I began to thank Jesus for the gifts that he gave me and I praised him for the gifts that he gave my brother seminarians. It was a very gradual and slow process, but Jesus showed me that when I am grateful for my own gifts, my own life, the need to compare goes away. When I thanked him for the gifts of my brothers and their talents, my heart was opened to love them more.

Remember *How the Grinch Stole Christmas*? It is envy that causes the Grinch to hate the Whos down in Whoville. These feelings of envy were first rooted in the Grinch's pride: "I am not satisfied in my Grinch-ness. I deserve better." As he looks down on Whoville, the Grinch resents the joy, peace, and love of the Whos. It takes an entire realignment of the Grinch's self-image, through their sharing and singing, to humble him and allow him to celebrate with them!

So, if you're feeling envious toward a friend, praise God for their gifts and allow Jesus to open up your heart to love. There is no reason to be envious. You are good, and it is *so good* that you exist!

LECTIO DIVINA

James 3:14–16

Who among you is wise and understanding? Let him show his works by a good life in the humility that comes from wisdom. But if you have bitter jealousy and selfish ambition in your hearts, do not boast and be false to the truth. Wisdom of this kind does not come down from above but is earthly, unspiritual, demonic. For where jealousy and selfish ambition exist, there is disorder and every foul practice.

IMAGINATIVE PRAYER

Think about a friend or a family member whom you may be envious of or have been in the past. What is the great gift or talent that they possess? What are you saying about yourself and your identity when you are resentful? How would you describe your feelings to Jesus? Can you thank Jesus and praise him for your friend's gift or talent?

JOURNALING

Use the space below to journal about your Holy Hour.

Day 10

WOUNDED?

By His Cross I Am Healed

The way of the Cross is the way of suffering. Christ
bore our sufferings and carried our sorrows. He was
wounded for our transgressions and bruised for our
iniquities. His wounds have healed us.

—St. John Vianney

Time for another superhero—this time, Iron Man. In the movies and comics, Tony Stark is a billionaire industrialist and genius inventor who creates a powerful suit of armor to fight crime and protect the world. However, he is also a very broken man. He is incredibly arrogant, proud, and vain; he is also a womanizer and an alcoholic. Stark possesses many wounds. Throughout the Marvel Universe, Stark's deep wounds cause him to lash out at the rest of the Avengers. They also manifest in Stark's great self-reliance and distrust of others.

So it is with the wounds we carry around from being hurt, abused, or traumatized: they cause negativity, anxiety, self-reliance, distrust, anger, and resentment. And if an emotional or spiritual wound is not healed, just like a physical wound, it will fester, grow, and cause other problems.

These wounding experiences don't necessarily have to be earth-shattering; they can be simple hurts. For example, when I was in college, I experienced a bit of bullying from other students in my major; they said I would never succeed in the field I was studying. A wound developed in my heart, and I

resolved never to show weakness in my studies and never again
to rely on others for help.

Tony Stark was wounded from the death of his parents and
vowed to do everything on his own. Stark's wound festered
with pride, self-reliance, and disrespect toward others. The
wound wasn't his fault, any more than the bullying I experienced was my fault—and the wound that is in your heart right
now isn't your fault!

Think of the wounds on Jesus's hands and feet and in his
side. They were not his fault, and his wounds redeemed our
woundedness, turning our feelings of defeat and pain into *victory*! When we give Jesus our wounds and are honest with him
about how we have been hurt, he can begin to heal and redeem
our pain. The more I gave my wound to Jesus and gave him
permission to heal me, the more that self-reliance dissolved.
Jesus is called the Divine Physician. Give him permission to
begin to heal your wounds.

LECTIO DIVINA

Matthew 8:1–15

When Jesus came down from the mountain, great crowds
followed him. And then a leper approached, did him hom-
age, and said, "Lord, if you wish, you can make me clean." He
stretched out his hand, touched him, and said, "I will do it. Be
made clean." His leprosy was cleansed immediately. Then Jesus
said to him, "See that you tell no one, but go show yourself to
the priest, and offer the gift that Moses prescribed; that will
be proof for them."

When he entered Capernaum, a centurion approached
him and appealed to him, saying, "Lord, my servant is lying at
home paralyzed, suffering dreadfully." He said to him, "I will
come and cure him." The centurion said in reply, "Lord, I am
not worthy to have you enter under my roof; only say the word

and my servant will be healed. For I too am a person subject to authority, with soldiers subject to me. And I say to one, 'Go,' and he goes; and to another, 'Come here,' and he comes; and to my slave, 'Do this,' and he does it." When Jesus heard this, he was amazed and said to those following him, "Amen, I say to you, in no one in Israel have I found such faith. I say to you, many will come from the east and the west, and will recline with Abraham, Isaac, and Jacob at the banquet in the kingdom of heaven, but the children of the kingdom will be driven out into the outer darkness, where there will be wailing and grinding of teeth." And Jesus said to the centurion, "You may go; as you have believed, let it be done for you." And at that very hour [his] servant was healed.

Jesus entered the house of Peter, and saw his mother-in-law lying in bed with a fever. He touched her hand, the fever left her, and she rose and waited on him.

IMAGINATIVE PRAYER

Matthew 8:1–15 recounts three different healings that Jesus performs. In whichever passage that strikes you the most, imagine yourself in the place of the one who needs healing. Bring to Jesus the wound that you are struggling with. Hear Jesus say to you, "This was not your fault." Imagine him healing you. Throughout the day, continue to give Jesus permission to heal your wounds.

JOURNALING

Use the space below to journal about your Holy Hour.

JESUS, I LOVE YOU.
PLEASE STRENGTHEN ME
The Next 10 Days

The next ten days move from the inside to the outside. Just as our interior life can prevent us from being fully alive, so can things from outside ourselves. External influences are all around us and prevent us from being the sons and daughters of God that we're called to be.

Most of these outside influences distract us from holiness. The seventeenth-century French philosopher Blaise Pascal said, "Without diversions we should be in a state of weariness, and this weariness would spur us to seek a more solid means of escaping from it. But diversion amuses us, and leads us unconsciously to death."[1] In other words, we distract ourselves from the abundant life and cling to the world, the flesh, and the devil. Time to kick the devil in the face and embrace Jesus Christ and the abundant life in these next ten days!

Day 11
FREEDOM FROM IDOLS
Am I Cheating You, God?

The greatest sin of our time is not the atomic bomb
or the unbridled greed which threatens to bankrupt
the world. It is the loss of faith, the darkening of the
human mind, the weakening of the will. The greatest
sin of our time is to reduce God to insignificance.

—St. Teresa of Calcutta

In the ancient world, Egyptians had their own pantheon of
gods, much like the Greeks. Each god represented a different
element of the world or human nature. Two of those gods that
have a small part to play in the salvation story are Apis and
Hathor. Apis, a god worshipped in the capital of ancient Egypt,
is depicted as a bull in artwork and statues. Hathor looked
like a cow and was worshipped for fertility, motherhood, and
the arts.

Remember the story of the golden calf in the book of
Exodus? The God of Israel, through Moses, frees the people
of Israel from slavery in Egypt. Moses then leads the people
through the desert for forty years to the Promised Land.
During the time in the desert, the people of Israel grow impa-
tient and build the golden calf. Have you ever wondered why
they chose a calf, of all things, to represent their rebellion?
Most likely it was Apis or Hathor!

The people of Israel were slaves in Egypt for over three
hundred years! That's longer than the United States has been
a country. Living in the Egyptian culture for that long . . .

73

of course they would have grown accustomed to the gods of Egypt. Apis and Hathor were familiar to them. So, what do you do when the strangeness of life kicks in and you just want to experience the comforts of home? Yep, you build a golden calf.

What do *we* do when we are scared, nervous, or fearful of the future? We cling to *what we know*. For such a long time, the Israelites clung to what they knew. It brought them comfort and security. That's idolatry in a nutshell. Here's what Pope Benedict XVI had to say about it:

> Idolatry is a subtle and insidious temptation, one that can easily creep into our lives and take root if we are not vigilant. It is a form of spiritual adultery, in which *we place our trust and devotion in something other than God.*[2]

Pope Benedict XVI reminds us that idolatry is like "spiritual adultery." We're cheating on God! Every time we choose a thing *over* God, we cheat on him. One of my good friends from college who is now married put it like this: "My wife and I love going to brunch together. I would brunch every day with her if I could. Wife + Brunch = Heaven. And God wants me and my wife to have brunch time. But if I choose to take my wife to brunch instead of Sunday Mass . . . I've made my wife an idol. I've made brunch an idol."

His example is a little bit goofy, but the reality is *good things* can become idols in our lives. Our family, our friends, our work, and so forth are all good things, but do they take the place of God? Is he the number one priority or is something else? Today during your Holy Hour, ask Jesus to reveal the idols in your life. Then ask him for courage not to cheat.

LECTIO DIVINA

Matthew 6:24

[Jesus said:] "No one can serve two masters. He will either hate one and love the other, or be devoted to one and despise the other. You cannot serve God and mammon."

Note: In this verse, "mammon" refers to wealth, material possessions, or money.

IMAGINATIVE PRAYER

In my work with college kids, I've noticed a trend in what truly becomes idols in the lives of young people. I've created a Top Ten list of idols that I see most often. Read the list, pray over the list, and see what strikes you. Tell Jesus about what idols you choose over him. Ask Jesus for freedom. Let Jesus love you.

Top Ten Idols (in alphabetical order)

- Ambition
- Body image
- Comfort (this is my biggest idol)
- Family
- Influencers
- Politics
- Pornography
- Social media footprint
- Sports
- Wokeness

JOURNALING

Use the space below to journal about your Holy Hour.

Day 12

WATCH YOUR ALGORITHM

Jesus, You Are My Treasure

For where your treasure is, there also will
your heart be.

—Matthew 6:21

Several months ago, I was at a large gathering of friends and
the topic of Instagram came up with a person who has been
in my life since childhood. He asked me if I could show him
the videos that I post on Instagram and handed me his phone.

You know how Instagram works . . . when you click on
"search," directly below the search bar there are all the square
images of things that you searched before—all your past search
results. So, if you are a gym rat, most likely a lot of images
of workout routines, fitness hacks, and before/after pics. If
you are a political junkie, most likely tons and tons of short
debate videos, news stories, and the ever-popular drop-the-mic
"burn" of a political opponent. If you are an animal lover, most
likely you have a search history of adorable kittens, puppies,
and hedgehogs dressed in costumes.

When I opened up this friend's Instagram account,
though, I saw bikinis. So. Many. Bikinis. There below the
search bar were sixteen squares of beautiful women with nothing on except bikinis.

My heart sank, and I honestly felt a little dizzy. This is a
good guy who has been a faithful friend all my life. I didn't
want to think about someone who I grew up with and have
seen mature and grow in virtue caught up in something

like this. And yet his algorithm (search history) revealed his struggle.

For so many young people, natural curiosity and our God-given desire for human connection can spiral into something much darker. When we give in to those temptations, they can trap us, creating wounds and spiritually toxic habits that can take a lifetime to eradicate and heal. Especially if we are already struggling with feelings of isolation and rejection, a few clicks can lead to addictions that change not only how we see others but also how we see ourselves. Lord, have mercy!

The algorithm is relentless. It reveals our hearts, what we desire, and what we are enslaved to. The more we feed it with new images or videos to satisfy our broken desires, the more the perpetual loop pulls us deeper and deeper into sin.

The good news: if you find yourself struggling with what the Bible calls "desires of the flesh," it is possible to change the algorithm! Social media is filled with good, true, and beautiful things that can lift our hearts to being fully alive. Search for those *transcendentals*. What channels on social media bring your heart closer to the Lord, closer to goodness and truth?

LECTIO DIVINA

Philippians 4:8–9

Finally, brothers, whatever is true, whatever is honorable, whatever is just, whatever is pure, whatever is lovely, whatever is gracious, if there is any excellence and if there is anything worthy of praise, think about these things. Keep on doing what you have learned and received and heard and seen in me. Then the God of peace will be with you.

IMAGINATIVE PRAYER

Imagine yourself in a comfortable place, a place that brings you peace. Imagine Jesus with you as you go through all your internet search history with him. What are you afraid to show him? How does Jesus look at you? How does he begin to heal you?

JOURNALING

Use the space below to journal about your Holy Hour.

Day 13

PORN ALERT!

Jesus, Teach Me to Crave Holiness

> The problem with pornography is not that it shows
> too much of the person, but that it shows far too little.
>
> —St. John Paul the Great

World Youth Day 2000 was held in a large open field outside
of Rome. That warm August afternoon, two million people
gathered to hear St. John Paul II speak to the young people
of the world. The Holy Father revealed the motto for the year,
"The Word was made flesh and dwelt among us." St. John
Paul II chose this theme after years of defending the dignity
of the flesh, especially when it came to the inhumanness of
pornography. In retrospect, we see the Holy Father's warning
proved timely. Seven years later, the largest and most popular
pornographic website, Pornhub, was founded, ensnaring even
the young by objectifying human intimacy.

Throughout his papacy, St. John Paul II anticipated other
future dangers that would lead to the degradation of human
dignity, all of which could be reduced to the tendency to consume and use rather than love and serve. In his book *Love
and Responsibility*, he wrote of the dignity that God the Father
instilled in each of us from the moment of our conception. It
is God who makes us worthy! You are worthy of love, not to
be used. But also you are called to love and not to use others.

In our culture, using and consuming has become a mindless pursuit. With a single click on our phone, every craving
is satisfied with a minimum of effort or social interaction,

from Amazon to Uber Eats. For those who recognize in themselves this preoccupation—even enslavement—to mindless consumption, there is so much hope! Jesus doesn't want you to be a slave. He wants you to be fully alive in him.

Before his conversion, St. Francis of Assisi was well known for his reckless, uncharitable behavior. St. Augustine also spoke about how he used and exploited women for his own pleasure. St. Mary of Egypt, before her conversion, used her beauty and sexual energy to seduce and manipulate men. Many other saints experienced these temptations to use and consume, but in time they changed. Today, praise God, they are in heaven, and there is hope for you! What did they have in common? The closer these saints grew in relationship with Jesus, the more they were able to cast off the sinful behaviors of the past. Stay close to Jesus, keep developing your relationship with him, and soon you will crave holiness, too!

LECTIO DIVINA

Matthew 11:28–30

Come to me, all you who labor and are burdened, and I will give you rest. Take my yoke upon you and learn from me, for I am meek and humble of heart; and you will find rest for yourselves. For my yoke is easy, and my burden light.

IMAGINATIVE PRAYER

If you are currently struggling with pornography, give Jesus permission into those shameful places. Allow Jesus to say to you, "I never wanted this for you." Ask him for freedom.

If you are not currently struggling with pornography, first pray for those who are. Second, call to mind other ways you may "consume" or "use" people, not treating them with the dignity they deserve. Imagine bringing those struggles to Jesus and ask him how to selflessly love those people you may use.

JOURNALING

Use the space below to journal about your Holy Hour.

Day 14

IT'S ALL ABOUT IMAGE

Jesus, Help Me Keep My Eyes on You

> The most powerful weapon to conquer the devil
> is humility. For as he does not know at all how to
> employ it, neither does he know how to defend him-
> self from it.

> —St. Vincent de Paul

I've been sober for six years . . . from social media. I used to be on everything from Snapchat to Instagram to Facebook to Twitter. What made me quit? Glad you asked.

A few months before my ordination to the priesthood, I was serving as the deacon at Mass. During the Eucharistic Prayer, as I stood next to the priest (and Jesus), I kept thinking about an Instagram post I had just made and how many comments there would be when I checked my phone after Mass. Seconds later I realized what I was doing and was ashamed of myself. Here I was, in the most precious moments of Mass, thinking about myself and my image. In that season of my life, I wanted to be "a man after God's heart," like King David. Instead I was acting very much like King Saul.

Remember King Saul, the first king of Israel, in the Old Testament? He was chosen by God to lead the Israelites and grow the kingdom of Israel. Saul was a good man with very good intentions. At first he was humble, obedient, God-fearing, and wise. Saul desired to do whatever was best for the people of Israel, and he strived to be a man of God. However, as time went on, Saul started looking to his own image rather than keeping his eyes on God.

In the first book of Samuel, chapter 15, Saul disobeys God's command to defend the people of Israel. Instead of destroying all the possessions of another tribe, he keeps all the possessions for himself. The prophet Samuel confronts him about his disobedience, but Saul denies that he did anything wrong. Doubling down on his disobedience, Saul then builds a monument to himself at Carmel (see 1 Sm 15:12)! Eventually Saul's self-centeredness and pride lead to his downfall. King Saul began with amazing, holy intentions to serve God's people as king. Slowly but surely, Saul's own image became his god.

Social media has many positive impacts, including communication, social connection, and support. But it can easily creep into an addiction to our own image. Keeping your eyes on your image is exhausting; keeping your eyes on God is freeing.

When I realized social media was distracting me during Mass, I thought to myself, "I am going to be a priest in a few months. I can't keep living like this. Jesus, I need to keep my eyes on you." So I went on my phone and uninstalled all my social media apps. Later that day I reinstalled them, deleted my actual accounts, and *then* uninstalled my apps.

Now, I'm not suggesting that this is the only way to win the social media battle. If you decide to start cutting down on social media, take it to prayer and consider discussing it with family and friends first. I will say, though, that the freedom I felt was unreal! All the pressure to curate my own image was gone!

Padre Pio famously said, "Let us fix our eyes on Jesus Christ and His most holy Mother, and fear nothing." Humility makes us like a child. A child is never concerned with their own image. They have complete faith and trust in their parents that they won't be judged. A child feels safe with their parents and can be free to live in the present moment.

LECTIO DIVINA

Matthew 18:1–5

At that time the disciples approached Jesus and said, "Who is the greatest in the kingdom of heaven?" He called a child over, placed it in their midst, and said, "Amen, I say to you, unless you turn and become like children, you will not enter the kingdom of heaven. Whoever humbles himself like this child is the greatest in the kingdom of heaven. And whoever receives one child such as this in my name receives me."

IMAGINATIVE PRAYER

Instead of admitting his mistakes, King Saul built a monument to himself; he was a slave to his own image. Are you ever tempted to build monuments to yourself? Humility is being like a child—safe and free, not concerned about their image. Imagine yourself as a child with God the Father. How do you feel? What is the experience of being a child with God the Father like?

JOURNALING

Use the space below to journal about your Holy Hour.

Day 15

DO YOU VALIDATE?

Jesus, Change Me

For to me life is Christ, and death is gain.
—Philippians 1:21

Many young people, looking for recognition and validation, are turning to social media to become "influencers" and to showcase their talents and personalities. In 2019, the Harris Poll found that 86 percent of teens (ages thirteen to seventeen) wanted to become influencers. The influencer lifestyle is seen as glamorous and fulfilling. Yet, behind the glamor and fame, many famous young influencers have expressed feelings of disillusionment and dissatisfaction with their online activities.

Essena O'Neill, a famous Instagram model and influencer, quit social media and began speaking out against the negative effects and toxic culture of the influencer lifestyle. Matilda Djerf, a Swedish fashion and travel influencer, announced a few years ago that she was quitting social media after experiencing panic and pressure to constantly create and maintain a perfect image. Others have experienced similar disillusionment, including Jameela Jamil, Chrissy Teigen, Tanya Burr, and Grant Gustin.

It turns out that being affirmed by random people online is only fulfilling for so long. Being affirmed by your heavenly Father for your goodness will last forever.

The greatest influencers the world has ever known are the saints. They literally changed the face of the earth! St. Ignatius of Loyola founded the Jesuit order that influenced education and missionary work throughout the globe. St. Teresa of Avila reformed the Carmelite order and changed the course of Church history in Spain forever. St. Catherine of Siena influenced Pope Gregory XI to return to Rome after living away for more than seventy years, which led to a renewal in Siena, Rome, and all of Italy. St. John Paul the Great's influence contributed to the fall of communism! The list of saint-influencers goes on and on. But the greatest difference between social media influencers and the saints is that social media influencers are self-focused, whereas the saints are Christ-focused. Through your witness to Jesus Christ, you are called to be a saint to change the course of history. Go forth and be an influencer for the Lord!

LECTIO DIVINA

Philippians 4:12–13

I know indeed how to live in humble circumstances; I know also how to live with abundance. In every circumstance and in all things I have learned the secret of being well fed and of going hungry, of living in abundance and of being in need. I have the strength for everything through him who empowers me.

IMAGINATIVE PRAYER

On your phone, use Google Images to search for the painting *Nebuchadnezzar* by William Blake. It is a famous and disturbing image of King Nebuchadnezzar, an Old Testament influencer who used his greatness, power, and fame to mold the Babylonian empire to his image and likeness. Everyone knew him, and everyone wanted to be him.

Refusing to honor the true and living God, Nebuchadnezzar was sentenced to "dwell with wild beasts . . . given grass to eat like an ox" (Dn 4:22). Now use Google Images to search for the face of St. Teresa of Calcutta. Notice, pray, and compare the difference between the world's influencers and Jesus Christ's influencers. Ask Jesus for the grace to be all for him!

JOURNALING

Use the space below to journal about your Holy Hour.

Day 16

VIDEO GAMES, VIRTUAL REALITY, AND AI

Jesus, What Do You Have for Me Now?

The secret of happiness is to live moment by moment
and to thank God for what He is sending us every
day in His goodness.

—**St. Gianna Molla**

In 2020, Pope Francis spoke like a champion, challenging young people to rise up:

> Today we are often "connected" but not communicating. The indiscriminate use of electronic devices can keep us constantly glued to the screen. With this Message, I would like to join you, young people, in calling for a cultural change, based on Jesus' command to "arise." In a culture that makes young people isolated and withdrawn into virtual worlds, let us spread Jesus' invitation: "Arise!" He calls us to embrace a reality that is so much more than virtual.[3]

Pope Francis wanted to emphasize the importance of living in the present moment and living in reality (which is Christ—the Way, the Truth, and the Life). Reality is true. Therefore, reality is Jesus.

When we "escape" from reality, we are also escaping from Jesus and what he desires for us in the present moment. That is exactly why video games, virtual reality, and artificial intelligence (AI) can be so dangerous. We get caught up in a world that is not real, and therefore we're disconnected from God.

I admittedly play video games, especially *Fortnite*, with my priest brothers. But there is a difference between video games as leisure and video games as an escape. In college I went through a tough breakup at one point, and instead of confronting my hurt feelings and healing from the experience, I escaped and spent hours bingeing role-playing games. I numbed myself and prevented the healing that Jesus desired for me.

Jesus is so real and so true that he wants us to live in the present moment with him. Video games are fun, and virtual reality can provide potential benefits to our culture, but please be "vigilant," as our Holy Father says, and stay with Jesus!

LECTIO DIVINA

John 8:31–32

Jesus then said to those Jews who believed in him, "If you remain in my word, you will truly be my disciples, and you will know the truth, and the truth will set you free."

IMAGINATIVE PRAYER

How do you escape reality? What in your heart are you trying to numb? What are the things you want to escape from? Can you share these things with Jesus? Imagine yourself with Jesus and his apostles. What do you think it was like for the apostles to always be with him? They never needed to "escape" because they were with him.

JOURNALING

Use the space below to journal about your Holy Hour.

Day 17

WHAT ABOUT ALCOHOL?

Jesus, Am I Giving Up True Freedom?

I would wish a great lake of beer for the King of
kings; I would wish the family of heaven to be drinking it throughout life and time.

—St. Brigid

Alcohol is a gift from God! Some of the best beer in the world
is made by Belgian monks. Some of the best wine in the world
is made by French Benedictines. Jesus's first miracle was turning water into wine. God made it good!

On the other hand, even good things can become prob-
lematic if we don't exercise good judgment. There's a difference between enjoying alcohol legally and in moderation and
sneaking off to get wasted (on your own or with friends). Have
you ever been at a party where you are the only one who is
sober? Yeah . . . it's uncomfortable: people acting weird and
making stupid decisions they'll regret later.

Alcohol is a social lubricant. It gives a false sense of reality
and false courage. Bottom line: drinking alcohol in excess robs
us of freedom and self-control, and easily leads to self-harm
and unforeseen consequences: unplanned pregnancies, abuse,
and accidents. And the more we justify our bad choices, the
further we get from God.

Recently one evening at the Newman Center, one of our
"Catholic 101" sessions was about what the Catholic Church
says about drinking. Olivia, one of our rock-star FOCUS

missionaries, shared her testimony about alcohol and drinking with all our students. I wanted to share her testimony.

> My freshman year of college, I wanted what everyone wanted—to have fun, feel free, and be liked. I wanted to be alive. I did this . . . by partying and drinking. I grew up in a very faithful home, so I knew I wanted to keep God close to me in college, but I thought every Catholic was doing what I was doing: partying on Saturday night and going to Mass on Sunday morning.
>
> This all changed when I started attending a weekly Bible study in my friend's dorm room. I knew something was different about these women the first day I showed up. I walked in barely knowing anyone, but these women quickly became my closest friends. They were filled with the joy of Christ! They prayed every day and encouraged me to do the same. I trusted these women, and I knew I'd have a better life if I did what they did. Although it took me a while—about two more years—I finally let go of my "double life" after realizing the "friends" I partied with didn't actually have my best interest in mind.
>
> I stopped the partying and dove into my faith. Through daily prayer and conversation with God, he showed me how in love with me he is. He showed me how vibrant my life could be with him. He showed me that the freedom I experience in him is so much more than what I was trying to imitate by drinking. Life with Jesus is everything I ever wanted: I am vibrant, I am free, and I am loved.

LECTIO DIVINA

Ephesians 5:18–19

And do not get drunk on wine, in which lies debauchery, but be filled with the Spirit, addressing one another [in] psalms and hymns and spiritual songs, singing and playing to the Lord in your hearts, giving thanks always and for everything in the name of our Lord Jesus Christ to God the Father.

IMAGINATIVE PRAYER

Do you tend to abuse alcohol? If so, what is the underlying desire that you are trying to self-medicate? Are you afraid? Feeling socially awkward?

Imagine the wedding at Cana. Imagine what drinking wine with Jesus, Mary, and the apostles might have looked like. Both his disciples and Olivia found freedom in the same place—not in alcohol but in Jesus. What does this say to you about your own attitude toward alcohol?

JOURNALING

Use the space below to journal about your Holy Hour.

Day 18

THE GOSSIP

Jesus, Be My Word of Life

> Gossip is a kind of murder. It kills people's reputations and, in many cases, their friendships and careers.
>
> —**St. Ignatius of Loyola**

One day St. Philip Neri was hearing confessions at his parish in Rome and a woman confessed to always falling into the sin of gossip. St. Philip said a few encouraging words and then gave her absolution and a very specific penance: she was to take a pillow up to the top of the church tower, rip open the pillow, and empty all the feathers out over the railing.

A few hours later the woman returned and said she had done what he asked. St. Philip then commanded her to go collect all the feathers. Greatly distressed, the woman respectfully told St. Philip, "Father, that's impossible! I will never be able to get back every single feather!" He responded, "So it is when you gossip and slander. The words that you say you can never take back."

Whether the story is historically accurate or an embellished account, St. Philip was making an important point about the dangers of gossip. Gossip is uncharitable conversation that can never be taken back. It tears down people, causes scandal, and leads to broken relationships. It is impossible to be a gossip and fully alive.

But if gossip is so sinful, why does it feel so good when we do it? Why do our worries seem to fade away when we are talking about someone else? Well, no one would ever sin if it didn't feel good, at least momentarily! Yet the reality is that even though gossip feels freeing for a moment, our hearts grow cold and thirsty after the temporary reprieve.

When we do not guard our lips out of love for the other, our hearts soon forget how to extend ourselves in acts of love. That is why one of the best antidotes for gossip is "seeing the other." We know the story of Adam and Eve. Adam is put into a deep sleep, and Eve is created out of Adam's rib. When Adam wakes up, he looks up and sees Eve. He is no longer living for himself; he is living for her! When we stop looking at ourselves and look up toward others—seeing others, loving others, and caring for others—we become more fulfilled.

Jesus Christ "looked up" in the most perfect way. He looked up, turned outward, and gave himself entirely for us. He is the perfect example of self-gift. The more we give ourselves away, the more fulfilled and satisfied we become.

LECTIO DIVINA

Luke 23:44–47

It was now about noon and darkness came over the whole land until three in the afternoon because of an eclipse of the sun. Then the veil of the temple was torn down the middle. Jesus cried out in a loud voice, "Father, into your hands I commend my spirit"; and when he had said this he breathed his last. The centurion who witnessed what had happened glorified God and said, "This man was innocent beyond doubt."

IMAGINATIVE PRAYER

Often when we fall into gossip, we have an unmet need inside of us. When I tear down someone else in order to build myself up, it may be because I feel I'm not good enough. I want an easy fix to feel as if I matter because deep down the lie that

I listen to is that I don't actually matter. Imagine yourself at the Cross with Jesus. Hear him tell you that you matter. You are enough.

JOURNALING

Use the space below to journal about your Holy Hour.

Day 19

MY LIFE PLAN

Show Me Your Will, O Lord

The will of God is not something to be feared but
something to be embraced. For when we do the
will of God, we find peace and joy that surpasses all
understanding.

—St. Gregory the Great

St. Gregory the Great was a Benedictine monk living in Rome
late in the sixth century AD. Gregory followed the Rule of St.
Benedict in the monastery and led a life of joyful humility. He
loved being a monk, and he was good at it! Gregory was living
his best life—praying all day, devoting himself to scripture,
and living simplicity. For Gregory, everything was awesome.

His life, however, changed drastically when, in AD 590,
Pope Pelagius II died during a plague that was sweeping
through Rome. Because of Gregory's holiness, the Church
looked to him to possibly be the next pope. Simple, intro-
verted, prayerful Gregory was very reluctant to accept the
position as pope. It would take away from his best life! The life
that he wanted was in the monastery, not in a public role of
administration. Gregory didn't feel qualified, and he wanted
to refuse the call from the Church. He even tried to flee Rome!

In the end, because Gregory was a prayerful man and loved
Jesus with his whole being, he couldn't impose his own will
when the "career" that he wanted was not what Jesus wanted.
Gregory said, "I have lost the peace of my monastic life and
am daily tormented by the burden of pastoral care. I wanted

to flee far away to hide from the burden of the pontificate, but I could not escape the hand of the Almighty."[1]

Gregory would be called Gregory the Great for what he did for Jesus and his Church. He became a respected and effective leader of the Catholic Church, and he worked tirelessly to reform issues in the Church. He also wrote extensively about a range of theological topics. Because of his previous life as a monk, Pope Gregory taught the world much about humility, detachment, and the desire for holiness.

St. Gregory the Great obviously had his own preference for his life and career. For us, especially those who are still working toward a career, the temptation can be strong to say to ourselves, "The career that I want is the only thing that will fulfill me!" Jesus, of course, desires you to thrive in your career and to honor God through your work, but is he part of the decision-making? Are you willing to surrender even your future to Jesus and say to him, "Not my will but yours be done" (Lk 22:42)?

LECTIO DIVINA

Mark 10:17–22

As he was setting out on a journey, a man ran up, knelt down before him, and asked him, "Good teacher, what must I do to inherit eternal life?" Jesus answered him, "Why do you call me good? No one is good but God alone. You know the commandments: 'You shall not kill; you shall not commit adultery; you shall not steal; you shall not bear false witness; you shall not defraud; honor your father and your mother.'" He replied and said to him, "Teacher, all of these I have observed from my youth." Jesus, looking at him, loved him and said to him, "You are lacking in one thing. Go, sell what you have, and give to [the] poor and you will have treasure in heaven; then come, follow me." At that statement his face fell, and he went away sad, for he had many possessions.

IMAGINATIVE PRAYER

For me, Mark 10:17–22 is such a sad scripture passage. Jesus specifically asks this young man for something, and he says no. The Lord invites the man to follow him, but in the end he refuses. Why would he ask a question if he wasn't ready for the answer?

When it comes to doing the will of God with our future, our vocation, and our career, are we ready for Jesus's answer? Imagine yourself in the place of the rich man. What does Jesus ask you to do? Are you free to say yes to him? Or are you forced to say no?

JOURNALING

Use the space below to journal about your Holy Hour.

Day 20

I AM NOT A COG

Whom Do You Say I Am, Lord?

You are not who they say you are, let me remind you of who you are!

—St. John Paul II to the people of Krakow, Poland

In 1979, St. John Paul II arrived in Krakow, Poland, to visit his homeland for the first time in his papacy. This took great courage because the Communist government still had a firm grip on Poland and was strictly aligned with the Soviet Union. The oppressive regime dictated that people were only good if they were useful; each person was to be like a cog in the machine, their worth measured strictly by what they were able to produce.

This papal visit was recognized as a direct challenge, a rallying cry to all those who were being oppressed. Like Katniss Everdeen in *The Hunger Games*, St. John Paul II announced to all the people gathered in Krakow that they were worth far more than they had been told. They were not cogs in a machine, worth nothing more than what they could produce. Rather, they were beloved sons and daughters of the Father.

The messaging we receive today is a bit different, but it is no less secular—and no less erroneous. Our culture tells us, "You don't have an identity! You have to make up your own identity!" Basically, "Figure it out for yourself; God has nothing to do with it." No wonder our culture experiences so much confusion, fear, and doubt when it comes to identity issues.

Then and now, St. John Paul the Great continues to speak the truth, which is the same today as it was in 1979. You are loved! You are God's! Your identity is that of a beloved son or daughter of the heavenly Father, and that will never be taken away from you! You are forever safe in this identity!

LECTIO DIVINA

John 15:15–16

"I no longer call you slaves, because a slave does not know what his master is doing. I have called you friends, because I have told you everything I have heard from my Father. It was not you who chose me, but I who chose you and appointed you to go and bear fruit that will remain, so that whatever you ask the Father in my name he may give you."

IMAGINATIVE PRAYER

While on the deepest level you are a son or daughter of God, we often become distracted by the messages that bombard us and cling to lesser identities:

I am what I do.
I am my physical appearance.
I am my grades at school.
I am my sexual orientation.
I am a failure and a sinner, unlovable and unloved.

Ask God to show you the truth. Let God the Father remind you of your true identity. You are not a cog. You are someone of infinite value, infinite worth, made in his divine image.

JOURNALING

Use the space below to journal about your Holy Hour.

JESUS, I WORSHIP YOU. THANKS FOR THE ABUNDANT LIFE

The Last 10 Days

Jesus promised us abundant life. The abundant life is him! And his abundant life is present to us in the Catholic Church. Within the Church, Jesus gave us everything we need to be fully alive in him.

This has been an exciting journey toward that "fully alive" experience Jesus wants for all of us. We spent the first ten days rejecting everything inside of us that is not consistent with the abundant life. After that, over the course of ten more days, we rejected outside influences that are not part of the abundant life. In these final ten days, we will embrace and celebrate the gifts that Jesus gave us through the Church so that we can have a taste of the abundant life we will fully experience when we are with him in heaven.

Are you ready to be fully alive?

Day 21

THE REAL PRESENCE OF THE EUCHARIST

Jesus Wants to Keep Me Close

The greatest love story of all time is contained in a tiny white host.

—**Archbishop Fulton Sheen**

When the pope travels to visit locations outside the Vatican, the Swiss Guard prepares for the pope's arrival by going through the building, making sure everything is secure. In the US, both the Secret Service and the Swiss Guard secure the locations. Often they'll use "detection dogs," which are known for finding hidden things, such as people hidden under the rubble of an earthquake.

When St. John Paul the Great visited California in 1987, his tour included a stop at Sacred Heart Preparatory Seminary in San Francisco. The Secret Service and Swiss Guard led detection dogs through the seminary to make certain no one was hiding, waiting to attack John Paul II. During the inspection, the detection dogs were led through the chapel, up and down the aisles, and into the confessionals.

As the Secret Service agents brought the detection dogs close to the sanctuary of the church, a remarkable thing happened: The detection dogs immediately stopped, became very still, and pointed their noses up to the tabernacle. The dogs had detected a presence: the Real Presence.

In the Eucharist, the God of the Universe makes himself available to us. He doesn't hide and is never far away. He wants to be so close that we receive his Body and Blood in Holy Communion! One of my students at the Newman Center posted on Instagram the GPS coordinates of the tabernacle in our chapel with the text "You can literally find God right here."

In Disney's *Hercules*, when the title character wants to talk to his dad, Zeus, he has to literally cross the country and climb a mountain to get his dad's attention. We can spend so much of our lives having that mindset . . . that Jesus is so distant from us. He's far away, and we have to clench our fists and pray *really hard* to get his attention. However, the Eucharist abolishes those lies! The Eucharist reveals the closeness of Jesus. You need him? He comes to you in the Holy Eucharist at every Mass. Our God wants to be close. Allow Jesus to get close to you. We can't hide from him!

LECTIO DIVINA

Psalm 139:4–5

Even before a word is on my tongue,
LORD, you know it all.

Behind and before you encircle me
and rest your hand upon me.

IMAGINATIVE PRAYER

When was the first time that you *knew* Jesus Christ was truly present in the Eucharist? How old were you? Where were you? What were your thoughts, feelings, and desires at the time?

JOURNALING

Use the space below to journal about your Holy Hour.

Day 22

EUCHARISTIC MIRACLES
Jesus Wants to Show Himself to Me

The Eucharist is my highway to heaven.

—**Blessed Carlos Acutis**

A few years ago, I led a group of high school students on a pilgrimage to Rome. Besides having perpetual anxiety from being in charge of the lives of fifteen minors in a foreign country, it was one of the most grace-filled seasons of my priesthood.

During one of the days of the pilgrimage, we traveled outside of Rome to the town of Orvieto. Orvieto is home to a Eucharistic miracle. For those who may not be aware, a Eucharistic miracle occurs when the flesh and blood of Jesus in the Eucharist, normally hidden from view, is revealed in a perceptible way to human senses. The appearance of bread and wine fades away, the veil is lifted, and the real presence of Jesus's flesh and blood is seen.

In 1263, in the town of Bolsena, Italy, the priest Dom Peter was celebrating Mass in Bolsena's parish church. During Mass, the priest was experiencing doubts about Jesus being truly present in the Eucharist. He wondered, "Is Jesus actually there? How is this not just a piece of bread?" During the consecration when Dom Peter said the words in Italian, "This is my Body," and elevated the host, he saw drops of blood fall from the consecrated host onto the corporal on the altar. This miracle brought Dom Peter's heart back to fully embracing the Church's teaching on the Eucharist. Pope Urban IV investigated this miracle and ordered that the blood-stained corporal be placed in the Orvieto Cathedral for public veneration. The Feast of Corpus Christi that we celebrate every year is because of what happened to Dom Peter in Bolsena.

I brought my students to Orvieto to see this blood-stained corporal, which remains in the church to this day. We celebrated Mass together there and spent our Holy Hour in front of the sacred relic. I will never forget what one of the teens said. He told me, "Fr. Tim, I totally get how amazing this miracle is, but I feel like the Eucharist in the tabernacle right now is even more amazing. Right?" When he said that, two things went through my mind. First was "He gets it!" Second was "Wow, this dude needs to be a priest." His insight was so beautiful because Eucharistic miracles reveal *what is already there!* Jesus sometimes allows the appearance of bread and wine to fade away so that we realize he has been there the whole time!

After our time in Orvieto, two of the students were so convicted that they began going to daily Mass. Both of them are now in college, and they continue to go to daily Mass and are absolutely *fully alive* because of their closeness to Jesus Christ in the Eucharist. The Eucharist is the source of our abundant life! The Church declares the Eucharist as the source and summit of our faith. We began this thirty-day Holy Hour adventure in order to become fully alive in Christ. Never forget: it all begins and ends with the Eucharist!

LECTIO DIVINA

John 6:48–59

"I am the bread of life. Your ancestors ate the manna in the desert, but they died; this is the bread that comes down from heaven so that one may eat it and not die. I am the living bread that came down from heaven; whoever eats this bread will live forever; and the bread that I will give is my flesh for the life of the world."

The Jews quarreled among themselves, saying, "How can this man give us [his] flesh to eat?" Jesus said to them, "Amen, amen, I say to you, unless you eat the flesh of the Son of Man and drink his blood, you do not have life within you. Whoever eats my flesh and drinks my blood has eternal life, and I will raise him on the last day. For my flesh is true food, and my blood is true drink. Whoever eats my flesh and drinks my blood remains in me and I in him. Just as the living Father sent me and I have life because of the Father, so also the one who feeds on me will have life because of me. This is the bread that came down from heaven. Unlike your ancestors who ate and still died, whoever eats this bread will live forever." These things he said while teaching in the synagogue in Capernaum.

IMAGINATIVE PRAYER

When Jesus made his presence known in the Eucharistic miracle in Bolsena, his blood dropped not only onto the corporal but also onto the marble floor. The blood penetrated and made an indentation in the marble. You can still see the indentation in the marble today, reminding us that the Eucharist can permeate even the hardest parts of our hearts.

What are the hardest parts of your heart? Where in your life do you keep Jesus out? What parts of your life do you refuse to trust Jesus with?

JOURNALING

Use the space below to journal about your Holy Hour.

Day 23

ADORATION

Jesus Really Likes Me!

Just as a mother loves her child not only when he is
good and lovable but even when he is wicked, so too
does Jesus love us in every situation. And he even
likes us, though we are nothing but sinners.

—St. Thérèse of Lisieux

This past November I had the privilege of witnessing my little
sister's marriage. Her wedding was the third happiest day of
my life, right behind my diaconate and priesthood ordinations.
I confess that I "ugly-cried" when my dad walked my sister,
Claire, down the aisle.

That day I noticed something about the bridal procession that I've never noticed before. When my sister was walking down the aisle with my dad, everyone stood up, turned
around, and looked at her . . . except for one group—the married women.

They were all looking at the groom. Instead of looking at
Claire, all the married women immediately looked at Mark. I
was fascinated and moved to see them so riveted by the ador-
ing gaze of love on Mark's face. They had all experienced this
look before when *they were the chosen one*, walking down the
aisle, having the love of their life adore them.

You know what? This is also how Jesus Christ looks at you
every time you go to adoration. Of course, *we* adore Our Lord
and Our God in the Blessed Sacrament, but *he adores us!* Jesus
Christ is gazing with love upon you!

Daughter of God, you are his beautiful bride, his precious creation. He regards you with the same understanding and compassion as he regarded the woman at the well, Mary and Martha, and his own mother. He revels in your femininity.

Son of God, Jesus looks at you with the same affection, the same infinite patience and understanding that he shared with Peter and the rest of the Twelve. He honors your masculinity.

St. Thérèse of Lisieux would go before the Blessed Sacrament, hold out her hands, and say, "Jesus! Love me as much as you want!" This bold prayer shows that she knew the truth that Jesus delighted in her and was perpetually gazing with love upon her.

We hear all the time in our religion classes, homilies, and sacramental preparation: Jesus loves you! And of course that's true. But what's more radical is that Jesus likes you! He delights in you. Jesus likes even the things that you may not like about your personality, your body, and your quirks. He likes those things.

Adoration is the most perfect time when we don't have to hide anything in shame. He is in the Blessed Sacrament right now, loving *and liking* you!

LECTIO DIVINA

Luke 10:21–22

At that very moment he rejoiced [in] the holy Spirit and said, "I give you praise, Father, Lord of heaven and earth, for although you have hidden these things from the wise and the learned you have revealed them to the childlike. Yes, Father, such has been your gracious will. All things have been handed over to me by my Father. No one knows who the Son is except the Father, and who the Father is except the Son and anyone to whom the Son wishes to reveal him."

IMAGINATIVE PRAYER

Read the scripture passage above and imagine the *joy* that Jesus is experiencing. He gives praise to the Father for having revealed his love to *you, his child*. Imagine how Jesus delights in you. What does he look like? How does he delight in you?

JOURNALING

Use the space below to journal about your Holy Hour.

Day 24

THE SACRED HEART

Give Me Your Heart, Jesus

The devotion to the Sacred Heart of Jesus is a source
of spiritual renewal and transformation, leading us
to greater union with God and a deeper love for our
neighbor.

—St. Teresa of Calcutta

In 1673, two days after Christmas, something incredible happened in Paray-le-Monial, France. Margaret Mary Alacoque, a twenty-six-year-old French nun, had a vision of Jesus that shocked and transformed how we see Jesus. This is what she wrote about the experience in her letters:

> [Jesus] asked me for my heart, which I begged Him to take. He did so and placed it in His own Adorable Heart, where He showed it to me as a little atom which was being consumed in this great furnace, and withdrawing it thence as a burning flame in the form of a heart, He restored it to the place whence He had taken it.

Jesus then spoke to her, saying,

> My well-beloved, I give you a precious token of My love, having enclosed within your side a little spark of its glowing flames, that may serve you for a heart and consume you to the last moment of your life.[1]

This rocks my socks every time I think about it! *God has a heart!* He isn't far away. He isn't distant. He came to us in

127

the Incarnation and literally had a physical heart. Image how Margaret Mary felt when she saw her own heart, how it was weak and not able to love and she wanted to love. All our hearts have weak spots. But Margaret Mary allowed Jesus to take her heart and place it in the heart of Jesus. And when she did, it was not destroyed. It became enflamed!

Think about the burning bush in the Old Testament. Moses sees the burning bush—it's ablaze but not consumed. The closer we get to the heart of Jesus, the more our hearts are enflamed with his love, yet they are not consumed.

In the Sacred Heart, Margaret Mary encountered perpetual love. She knew she couldn't love as she wanted to love, but with Jesus she was able to love heroically. And so can you!

LECTIO DIVINA

Ephesians 3:14–21

For this reason I kneel before the Father, from whom every family in heaven and on earth is named, that he may grant you in accord with the riches of his glory to be strengthened with power through his Spirit in the inner self, and that Christ may dwell in your hearts through faith; that you, rooted and grounded in love, may have strength to comprehend with all the holy ones what is the breadth and length and height and depth, and to know the love of Christ that surpasses knowledge, so that you may be filled with all the fullness of God.

Now to him who is able to accomplish far more than all we ask or imagine, by the power at work within us, to him be glory in the church and in Christ Jesus to all generations, forever and ever. Amen.

IMAGINATIVE PRAYER

Use Google Images to search for "Sacred Heart of Jesus." Scroll through the images and find one that speaks to you the most.

Look at how his heart is ablaze but not destroyed. Look at the wound in his heart. Imagine your own heart: What does it look like? Where are the weak spots? How are you not able to love as you want to love? Imagine yourself with Jesus. What does he do with your heart?

JOURNALING

Use the space below to journal about your Holy Hour.

Day 25

THE IMMACULATE HEART
OF MARY

Can I Trust God in the Pain?

Mary's Immaculate Heart reveals to us the love of
God which restores human beings to the dignity of
children of God, created in his image and likeness.
The heart of a mother is always united to the heart of
her child, and Mary's heart is united to the heart of
Christ, her Son, in the work of our redemption.

—St. John Paul the Great

One of my favorite chapels of all time is in my hometown of
Mundelein. The chapel is attached to the National Shrine of
St. Maximilian Kolbe. It is a small chapel inside of a bigger
chapel—the Sorrowful Mother Chapel. Growing up, I spent
hours and hours in that small, beautiful chapel dedicated to
Mary, praying about my vocation.

I was always drawn to a mosaic of Mary's heart on the
front of the altar. The mosaic was an image of the Immaculate
Heart of Mary. The image shows a burning heart with flames
coming from the top of Mary's heart. Seven swords are pierc-
ing her heart. I was fascinated with these swords, recalling the
scripture about this image. Simeon says to Mary,

> Behold, this child is destined for the fall and rise of many
> in Israel, and to be a sign that will be contradicted (and you

131

yourself a sword will pierce) so that the thoughts of many hearts may be revealed. (Lk 2:34–35)

As I thought about my future vocation, many fears crept in, causing a lot of hurt and pain in my heart. It brought me comfort knowing that Mary had hurt and pain, too—pain that actually pierced her heart like a sword. Yet Mary never doubted the Father's love and will for her, whereas I *frequently* doubted the Father's love for me: "Heavenly Father, can I actually trust you that you want the best for me? That I'll be happy?"

Praise God, after five years as a priest of Jesus Christ, the Father has been absolutely faithful to his promises for me. He's always wanted the best for me. And every year of my priesthood I've been happier! The Immaculate Heart of Mary taught me that I can experience pain, but I can trust completely in God in the midst of the pain.

LECTIO DIVINA

Luke 2:22–35

When the days were completed for their purification according to the law of Moses, they took him up to Jerusalem to present him to the Lord, just as it is written in the law of the Lord, "Every male that opens the womb shall be consecrated to the Lord," and to offer the sacrifice of "a pair of turtledoves or two young pigeons," in accordance with the dictate in the law of the Lord.

Now there was a man in Jerusalem whose name was Simeon. This man was righteous and devout, awaiting the consolation of Israel, and the holy Spirit was upon him. It had been revealed to him by the holy Spirit that he should not see death before he had seen the Messiah of the Lord. He came in the Spirit into the temple; and when the parents brought in the child Jesus to perform the custom of the law in regard to him, he took him into his arms and blessed God, saying:

"Now, Master, you may let your servant go
        in peace, according to your word,
for my eyes have seen your salvation,
        which you prepared in sight of all the peoples,
a light for revelation to the Gentiles,
        and glory for your people Israel."

The child's father and mother were amazed at what was said about him; and Simeon blessed them and said to Mary his mother, "Behold, this child is destined for the fall and rise of many in Israel, and to be a sign that will be contradicted (and you yourself a sword will pierce) so that the thoughts of many hearts may be revealed."

IMAGINATIVE PRAYER

Use Google Images to search for a picture of the Immaculate Heart of Mary. Choose one that resonates with your own heart. What strikes you about the image? What is Mary revealing to you about herself? About her son?

JOURNALING

Use the space below to journal about your Holy Hour.

Day 26

MARY, THE UNTIER OF KNOTS
I Can Find Freedom in Our Lady

The knot of disobedience of our first parents was
untied by the obedience of Jesus, the new Adam. And
if the ancient serpent, the devil, tempted the woman
to distance herself from God's plan, Mary, the new
Eve, unites herself to God's plan with her "yes."

—His Holiness Pope Francis

In 2016 I got a personal "pep talk" from Pope Francis! The
day before my diaconate ordination, he met with my deacon
class in St. Peter's Square to pray over us and give us some
fatherly words of wisdom. After he prayed over us, he said
very simply in his broken English, "Stay close to Mary. Pray
to Mary every day. Pray the Rosary every day. Stay close to
her." Very simple but exactly what my heart needed to hear!
Pope Francis has a great devotion to Mary, and the passion in
which he urged us to stay close to Mary was obviously born
of his own experience.

Pope Francis has a special devotion to a particular image
of Mary that is becoming more and more popular. Before
he was pope, during his time in Germany, he came across
Mary, Untier of Knots, a painting by Johann Georg Melchior
Schmidtner. The painting depicts angels holding up a ribbon
and Mary untying knots in the ribbon. The knots represent the
sins, addictions, and struggles we face in our lives. Through
Mary's intercession and fierce help, we can be released from

those sins and addictions and become free! Pope Francis said in his audience on October 12, 2013,

> Mary, whose "yes" opened the door for God to undo the knot of the ancient disobedience, is the Mother who patiently and lovingly brings us to God, so that he can untangle the knots of our soul by his fatherly mercy.[2]

All healing and freedom ultimately come from Jesus Christ, but we can have full confidence in surrendering these "knots" to Our Lady! Mary's intercession leads us from slaves to freedom!

LECTIO DIVINA

Revelation 12:1–6

A great sign appeared in the sky, a woman clothed with the sun, with the moon under her feet, and on her head a crown of twelve stars. She was with child and wailed aloud in pain as she labored to give birth. Then another sign appeared in the sky; it was a huge red dragon, with seven heads and ten horns, and on its heads were seven diadems. Its tail swept away a third of the stars in the sky and hurled them down to the earth. Then the dragon stood before the woman about to give birth, to devour her child when she gave birth. She gave birth to a son, a male child, destined to rule all the nations with an iron rod. Her child was caught up to God and his throne. The woman herself fled into the desert where she had a place prepared by God, that there she might be taken care of for twelve hundred and sixty days.

IMAGINATIVE PRAYER

Imagine the tightest knots in your life right now. Maybe it's a sin, an addiction, a trauma, a doubt . . . Whatever it is, imagine giving those knots to Mary. What does she do? How does she look at you? How do Mary and Jesus help you to go from slavery to freedom?

JOURNALING

Use the space below to journal about your Holy Hour.

Day 27

APOSTOLIC SUCCESSION

Jesus, Stay with Me, Your Sheep

> Wherever the bishop shall appear, there let the
> multitude also be: even as, wherever Jesus Christ is,
> there is the Catholic Church.
>
> **—St. Ignatius of Antioch**

When I received the Sacrament of Confirmation in eighth
grade, our bishop explained apostolic succession to us: he
had been ordained by a bishop, who had been ordained by a
bishop, who was ordained by his bishop . . . all the way to the
twelve apostles!

I remember at that time two emotions stirred in my heart.
First, I felt *reverence*. The man standing in front of me is literally one of the apostles! His authority had been passed from
one generation to the next, very much like a baton relay race.
Each "runner" bears the authority and responsibility for leading the team to the finish line. This unbroken chain of grace
was in this bishop who was about to confirm me. This reality
helped me to enter into my Confirmation in a deeper, more
awe-filled way.

The second emotion I experienced was *safety*, knowing
that Jesus has protected his Church for so long. If you've ever
been to St. Peter's Square in Rome or have seen a picture of
the square from above, you'll notice that the outside barrier
of the square looks like arms. This is an image of the Church
drawing her children into her embrace and keeping them safe
from the outside dangers of the world. Within the Church we

have the Eucharist, the forgiveness of sins, and the promise of eternal life with Jesus! I think a saint, pope, and holy person said this, but there is no place in the world safer than within the one, holy Catholic and apostolic Church!

LECTIO DIVINA

John 20:19–23

On the evening of that first day of the week, when the doors were locked, where the disciples were, for fear of the Jews, Jesus came and stood in their midst and said to them, "Peace be with you." When he had said this, he showed them his hands and his side. The disciples rejoiced when they saw the Lord. [Jesus] said to them again, "Peace be with you. As the Father has sent me, so I send you." And when he had said this, he breathed on them and said to them, "Receive the holy Spirit. Whose sins you forgive are forgiven them, and whose sins you retain are retained."

IMAGINATIVE PRAYER

Imagine the places in your life where you feel the most unsafe. Imagine how Jesus, through the Church, can help you feel safe and secure. Share your feelings of safety or lack of safety with Jesus. How does he respond?

JOURNALING

Use the space below to journal about your Holy Hour.

Day 28

REDEMPTIVE SUFFERING

My Suffering Can Change the World

Suffering is the nourishment of the love which has died to all that is merely human and has risen to a new life in Christ.

—St. Teresa Benedicta of the Cross (Edith Stein)

You've probably heard the phrase "Offer it up" before. Got a paper cut? Offer it up! Have a sore throat? Offer it up! Can't fall asleep? Offer it up! It is counterproductive and not helpful to hear the phrase "Offer it up" when we are in the midst of some kind of suffering. When we are suffering, we don't need a phrase—we need a person! We need someone to comfort us and be with us in our suffering. The Church from the very beginning has given us, through Jesus, the concept of redemptive suffering.

The most horrible moment of human history was the Crucifixion: God who suffered and died. But the same moment is the greatest moment: our redemption! Jesus Christ transforms suffering into something good! When we unite our suffering with Jesus, he can transform it into something good and redemptive. Our suffering as Christians isn't just something that hurts; our suffering can change the world. Through Jesus, our suffering brings grace, transformation, and redemption. You look at the lives of the saints and the one thing that they all have in common is that through Jesus their suffering *meant something*.

In his famous letter *Salvifici Doloris* (*On the Christian Meaning of Human Suffering*), St. John Paul II tells us that our suffering has meaning. "In bringing about the Redemption through suffering, Christ *has* also *raised human suffering to the level of the Redemption.* Thus each man, in his suffering, can also become a sharer in the redemptive suffering of Christ."[3] Uniting our personal suffering with Christ's "open[s] the way to the victory" of Christ's salvation.[4] What a message! Suffering with Jesus can change the world! If you are currently suffering in any way, it doesn't have to be meaningless. Please don't be afraid. Give permission for Jesus to use your suffering. Give permission for Jesus to be with you in your suffering.

LECTIO DIVINA

John 11:1–44

Now a man was ill, Lazarus from Bethany, the village of Mary and her sister Martha. Mary was the one who had anointed the Lord with perfumed oil and dried his feet with her hair; it was her brother Lazarus who was ill. So the sisters sent word to him, saying, "Master, the one you love is ill." When Jesus heard this he said, "This illness is not to end in death, but is for the glory of God, that the Son of God may be glorified through it." Now Jesus loved Martha and her sister and Lazarus. So when he heard that he was ill, he remained for two days in the place where he was. Then after this he said to his disciples, "Let us go back to Judea." The disciples said to him, "Rabbi, the Jews were just trying to stone you, and you want to go back there?" Jesus answered, "Are there not twelve hours in a day? If one walks during the day, he does not stumble, because he sees the light of this world. But if one walks at night, he stumbles, because the light is not in him." He said this, and then told them, "Our friend Lazarus is asleep, but I am going to awaken him." So the disciples said to him, "Master, if he is asleep, he will be saved." But Jesus was talking about his death, while they thought that he meant ordinary sleep. So then Jesus said to them clearly, "Lazarus has died. And I am glad for you that I was not there, that you may believe. Let us go to him." So Thomas, called Didymus, said to his fellow disciples, "Let us also go to die with him."

When Jesus arrived, he found that Lazarus had already been in the tomb for four days. Now Bethany was near Jerusalem, only about two miles away. And many of the Jews had come to Martha and Mary to comfort them about their brother. When Martha heard that Jesus was coming, she went to meet him; but Mary sat at home. Martha said to Jesus, "Lord, if you had been here, my brother would not have died. [But] even now I know that whatever you ask of God, God will give you." Jesus said to her, "Your brother will rise." Martha said to him, "I know he will rise, in the resurrection on the last day." Jesus told her, "I am the resurrection and the life; whoever believes in me, even if he dies, will live, and everyone who lives and believes in me will never die. Do you believe this?" She said to him, "Yes, Lord. I have come to believe that you are the Messiah, the Son of God, the one who is coming into the world."

When she had said this, she went and called her sister Mary secretly, saying, "The teacher is here and is asking for you." As soon as she heard this, she rose quickly and went to him. For Jesus had not yet come into the village, but was still where Martha had met him. So when the Jews who were with her in the house comforting her saw Mary get up quickly and go out, they followed her, presuming that she was going to the tomb to weep there. When Mary came to where Jesus was and saw him, she fell at his feet and said to him, "Lord, if you had been here, my brother would not have died." When Jesus saw her weeping and the Jews who had come with her weeping, he became perturbed and deeply troubled, and said, "Where have you laid him?" They said to him, "Sir, come and see." And Jesus wept. So the Jews said, "See how he loved him." But some of them said, "Could not the one who opened the eyes of the blind man have done something so that this man would not have died?"

So Jesus, perturbed again, came to the tomb. It was a cave, and a stone lay across it. Jesus said, "Take away the stone." Martha, the dead man's sister, said to him, "Lord, by now there will be a stench; he has been dead for four days." Jesus said to her, "Did I not tell you that if you believe you will see the glory of God?" So they took away the stone. And Jesus raised his eyes and said, "Father, I thank you for hearing me. I know that you always hear me; but because of the crowd here I have said this, that they may believe that you sent me." And when he had said this, he cried out in a loud voice, "Lazarus, come out!" The dead man came out, tied hand and foot with burial bands, and his face was wrapped in a cloth. So Jesus said to them, "Untie him and let him go."

IMAGINATIVE PRAYER

Place yourself in the scene with Jesus at Lazarus's tomb. Pay special attention to verse 35. Imagine Jesus weeping with you in your pain and suffering. Jesus hurts when you hurt. His love for you is personal.

JOURNALING

Use the space below to journal about your Holy Hour.

Day 29

THE RESURRECTION

Jesus, Let Your Spirit Arise in Me

Without the resurrection, human life would be incomprehensible; it would be without hope and without meaning.

—Pope Benedict XVI

He is risen! These three words echo throughout all of human history. Everything that we know and understand and believe is founded upon the truth of these three words. Nothing about our lives makes sense without them. With them, everything means something!

Think about how this theme plays out in your favorite movies. Here are some classics to get you started. Without Anna and her sacrifice, *Frozen* wouldn't make any sense. Without Eleven and her telepathy, *Stranger Things* wouldn't make sense. And without Bilbo and the Ring, *Lord of the Rings* wouldn't make sense. Without Jesus and his resurrection, our story makes no sense. The Resurrection is not just a historical fact but a living reality!

Jesus Christ is victorious over sin and death! He is victorious over all the sins, wounds, shame, and weakness of your heart. You never have to be afraid again.

LECTIO DIVINA

John 20:1–18

On the first day of the week, Mary of Magdala came to the tomb early in the morning, while it was still dark, and saw the stone removed from the tomb. So she ran and went to Simon Peter and to the other disciple whom Jesus loved, and told them, "They have taken the Lord from the tomb, and we don't know where they put him." So Peter and the other disciple went out and came to the tomb. They both ran, but the other disciple ran faster than Peter and arrived at the tomb first; he bent down and saw the burial cloths there, but did not go in. When Simon Peter arrived after him, he went into the tomb and saw the burial cloths there, and the cloth that had covered his head, not with the burial cloths but rolled up in a separate place. Then the other disciple also went in, the one who had arrived at the tomb first, and he saw and believed. For they did not yet understand the scripture that he had to rise from the dead. Then the disciples returned home.

But Mary stayed outside the tomb weeping. And as she wept, she bent over into the tomb and saw two angels in white sitting there, one at the head and one at the feet where the body of Jesus had been. And they said to her, "Woman, why are you weeping?" She said to them, "They have taken my Lord, and I don't know where they laid him." When she had said this, she turned around and saw Jesus there, but did not know it was Jesus. Jesus said to her, "Woman, why are you weeping? Whom are you looking for?" She thought it was the gardener and said to him, "Sir, if you carried him away, tell me where you laid him, and I will take him." Jesus said to her, "Mary!" She turned and said to him in Hebrew, "Rabbouni," which means Teacher. Jesus said to her, "Stop holding on to me, for I have not yet ascended to the Father. But go to my brothers and tell them, 'I am going to my Father and your Father, to my

God and your God.'" Mary of Magdala went and announced to the disciples, "I have seen the Lord," and what he told her.

IMAGINATIVE PRAYER

How does the Resurrection affect your story? During these twenty-nine days, you have grown to know the heart of the Lord. My invitation for you during this Holy Hour is to go through your own story. Go through the most significant moments of your life: your joys, sorrows, hurts, and wins. Invite Jesus into those moments. Allow Jesus to redeem your story through his resurrection.

JOURNALING

Use the space below to journal about your Holy Hour.

Day 30

THE ABUNDANT LIFE

Jesus, Make Me Fully Alive!

The glory of God is man fully alive!

—**St. Irenaeus**

Wow! Thirty days! Seven hundred and twenty hours! Forty-three thousand two minutes! This is the amount of time it takes to walk from Las Vegas to New York. It's the amount of time it takes to watch the entire series of *The Office* on repeat nine times. But for this amount of time, you decided to commit to divine intimacy with the Lord! Praise God for everything he's been doing in your heart!

I hope you've experienced what it means to be fully alive in Jesus. I hope you've discovered the authentic and unique relationship that God wants specifically with you. I hope you've experienced healing, freedom, joy, peace, and *life*. Remember what Jesus said: "The thief comes only to steal and slaughter and destroy; I came so that they might have life and have it more abundantly" (Jn 10:10). The thief, the evil one, wants to cause division and confusion in your heart. The fruits of the thief are fear, anxiety, division, confusion, and unrest. Reject these fruits! Embrace the promise of Jesus and the fruits of his Spirit: peace, consolation, joy, freedom, tranquility, love, and selflessness.

A daily Holy Hour changed my life and has changed the lives of many of my students. You were made for the Holy Hour. You were made for that intentional time spent with Jesus Christ. Any time spent with the Lord is never in vain and never wasted. Our hearts keep going deeper with our Creator, and it never ends, not even when we get to heaven!

I want to leave you with my favorite prayer, the Anima Christi, that I pray daily. I love you. I'm praying for you. Please stay close to Jesus!

> Soul of Christ, sanctify me.
> Body of Christ, save me.
> Blood of Christ, inebriate me.
> Water from the side of Christ, wash me.
> Passion of Christ, strengthen me.
> O good Jesus, hear me.
> Within your wounds hide me.
> And suffer me not to be separated from thee.
> From the malignant enemy, defend me.
> And at the hour of my death, call me
> and bid me to come to thee
> that with all thy angels and saints I may praise you
> forever and ever.
> Amen.

LECTIO DIVINA

Acts 2:42–47

They devoted themselves to the teaching of the apostles and to the communal life, to the breaking of the bread and to the prayers. Awe came upon everyone, and many wonders and signs were done through the apostles. All who believed were together and had all things in common; they would sell their property and possessions and divide them among all according to each one's need. Every day they devoted themselves to meeting together in the temple area and to breaking bread in their homes. They ate their meals with exultation and sincerity of heart, praising God and enjoying favor with all the people.

And every day the Lord added to their number those who were being saved.

IMAGINATIVE PRAYER

God gave us the great gift of memory. In moments of desolation, we can look back at times of consolation. Look back at these thirty days with Jesus. What special grace moments from your Holy Hours does Jesus want you to remember? Spend time going through your journal and express gratitude to God. The graces you received during these thirty days were real! Never forget!

JOURNALING

Use the space below to journal about your Holy Hour.

CONCLUSION

Bill Belichick, the head coach of the New England Patriots, is considered one of the best NFL coaches of all time. One of his claims to fame is the importance he places on what happens after the game. Belichick is so successful because he puts meticulous attention and detail into post-game analysis. With his team he thoroughly reviews game footage, where he identifies strengths, weaknesses, and areas for improvement. Commentators and fans attribute a great portion of the Patriots' success to the post-game analysis.

Our thirty-day journey together has been filled with grace and experiences of the Lord's love. However, as important as our Holy Hours have been, our post-prayer analysis is just as important. Prayer *is* our relationship with Jesus, and after thirty days we can begin to analyze our strengths, weaknesses, and areas for improvement in our prayer.

Remember, there are no "life hacks" with prayer. The Holy Spirit is the one who prays within us, and we can't "hack" God. However, as human beings, we can grow stronger and more faithful in our prayer life and more open to receiving all the graces that the Holy Spirit wants to give us!

Here are some prompts to help you journal your post-prayer analysis:

- The greatest grace I received as I made these Holy Hours was _____.

- I want to carry this great grace in my heart and always remember it by _____.

- I encountered Jesus Christ in a new way when _____.

- I learned this about my own heart in my Holy Hour:
  _____.
- During my Holy Hours I was at my best when
  _____.
- I was most distracted in my Holy Hours when
  _____.
- My favorite part of Holy Hour was _____.
- The most difficult part of Holy Hour was _____.
- Of the "three approaches" to prayer (lectio divina, imaginative prayer, and journaling prayer), the one that helped me the most was _____.
- I encountered Jesus in lectio divina when _____.
- I encountered Jesus in imaginative prayer in a significant way when _____.
- Journaling helped me by _____.
- One Holy Hour experience that I want to share is
  _____.

GREAT WAYS TO KEEP YOUR HOLY HOUR HABIT GOING AND GROWING!

If you have made it your goal to keep your "Holy Hour habit," that's great! Below are some good ways to make meeting up with Jesus in adoration an important part of your spiritual life. In addition, if you particularly enjoy prayer journaling, you might want to check out *The Ave Prayer Intentions Journal* or some of the other resources listed at the back of this book. Above all, stay close to the Sacred Heart of Jesus and the Immaculate Heart of Mary! Here are ten good ways to do this:

1. Prioritize Jesus and your prayer above everything else.

2. Add your prayer time/Holy Hour into your calendar.

3. If possible (even if it's a little inconvenient), attend daily Mass.

4. Go to Confession once a month.

5. Use the gospel of the day for daily lectio divina.

6. Use the gospel of the day for imaginative prayer.

7. Visit Jesus in the Eucharist often and let him love you.

8. Get a copy of this book for the person in your life who you think needs it the most, and pray for them!

9. Pray the Rosary and Divine Mercy Chaplet. (If you're not sure how to do this, pick up a copy of *The Ave Treasury of Catholic Prayers*.)

10. Make a daily examen before bed.

To make a daily examen, just place yourself in the presence of God before you go to bed and ask yourself:

- When was God's presence most acutely felt in my life today?
- For what moment (or moments) am I most thankful?
- In what ways have my emotions affected my choices today?
- Can I recall anything I need to forgive or for which I need forgiveness?
- As I anticipate tomorrow, where do I especially need God's presence?

From *The Ave Treasury of Catholic Prayers*

NOTES

Foreword

1. Francis, "Homily for XXXVII World Youth Day," Lisbon, Portugal, August 2, 2023, Vatican website, https://www.vatican.va/content/francesco/en/homilies/2023/documents/20230802-portogallo-omelia.html.

How Do I Make a Holy Hour?

1. Fulton Sheen, *Treasure in Clay* (New York: Image, 1982), 202.

2. Sheen, *Treasure in Clay*, 199.

3. Alphonsus Liguori, *Visits to the Blessed Sacrament* (Charlotte, NC: TAN Books, 2001), 9.

4. Francis, "General Audience," speech, October 18, 2023, https://www.vatican.va/content/francesco/en/audiences/2023/documents/20231018-udienza-generale.html.

5. Francis, "Address of His Holiness Pope Francis to Participants in the General Chapters of the Order of the Most Holy Savior of Saint Bridget and the Comboni Missionary Sisters," speech, October 22, 2022, Vatican website, https://www.vatican.va/content/francesco/en/speeches/2022/october/documents/20221022-capitoli-generali.html.

6. Benedict XVI, *Sacramentum Caritatis* (*On the Eucharist as the Source and Summit of the Church's Life and Mission*), February 22, 2007, Vatican website, para. 14, https://www.vatican.va/content/benedict-xvi/en/apost_exhortations/documents/hf_ben-xvi_exh_20070222_sacramentum-caritatis.html.

7. Francis, "General Audience," speech, October 18, 2023, https://www.vatican.va/content/francesco/en/audiences/2023/documents/20231018-udienza-generale.html

8. John Paul II, *Ecclesia de Eucharistia* (*On the Eucharist and Its Relationship to the Church*), April 17, 2003, Vatican website, para. 25, https://www.vatican.va/content/john-paul-ii/en/encyclicals/documents/hf_jp-ii_enc_20030417_eccl-de-euch.html

9. Robert Sarah, *The Power of Silence: Against the Dictatorship of Noise* (San Francisco: Ignatius Press, 2017), 32.

10. Benedict XVI, "General Audience," Castel Gandolfo, Italy, August 10, 2011, Vatican website, https://www.vatican.va/content/benedict-xvi/en/audiences/2011/documents/hf_ben-xvi_aud_20110810.html.

11. Robert Barron, "Bishop Barron on How to Read the Bible," Bishop Robert Barron, YouTube video, 7:39, April 11, 2011, https://www.youtube.com/watch?v=Ha5flTRTZWY&t=7s.

12. Jeremy Sutton, "5 Benefits of Journaling for Mental Health," PositivePsychology.com, February 9, 2023, https://positivepsychology.com/benefits-of-journaling.

Meeting Jesus Where I Need Him Most: The Thirty Days

1. Daniel Coyle, *The Talent Code: Greatness Isn't Born. It's Grown. Here's How* (New York: Bantam Books, 2009), 87.

Jesus, I Need You. Please Help Me: The First 10 Days

1. Martin Grabmann, *The Interior Life of St. Thomas Aquinas* (Milwaukee, WI: Bruce Publishing Company, 1951), 60.

2. *Captain America: The First Avenger*, directed by Joe Johnston (Burbank, CA: Marvel Studios, 2011).

3. "Tom Brady on Winning: There's "'Got to Be More Than This,'" *60 Minutes*, January 30, 2019, YouTube video, 1:08, https://www.youtube.com/watch?v=-TA4_fVkv3c.

4. Augustine, *The Confessions*, trans. Maria Boulding (Hyde Park, NY: Ignatius Press, 2001), 19.

5. Royal Society for Public Health, *#StatusOfMind: Social Media and Young People's Mental Health and Wellbeing*, May 2017, https://www.rsph.org.uk/our-work/campaigns/status-of-mind.html.

6. McLean Hospital, "The Social Dilemma: Social Media and Your Mental Health," McLeanHospital.org, January 18, 2023, https://www.mcleanhospital.org/essential/it-or-not-social-medias-affecting-your-mental-health.

7. Thérèse of Lisieux, *Story of a Soul: The Autobiography of St. Thérèse of Lisieux*, trans. John Clarke (Washington, DC: ICS Publications, 1996), 20.

8. *The Martian*, directed by Ridley Scott (Los Angeles: Twentieth Century Fox, 2015). See also Andy Weir, *The Martian* (New York: Crown, 2011).

9. Thomas Aquinas, *Summa Theologiae*, trans. the Fathers of the English Dominican Province (Notre Dame, IN: Christian Classics, 1981), II-II, 36,1.

Jesus, I Love You. Please Strengthen Me: The Next 10 Days

1. Blaise Pascal, *Pensées*, trans. A. J. Krailheimer (New York: Penguin Classics, 1995), sec. 171.

2. Benedict XVI, "Homily of His Holiness Benedict XVI," Vatican Basilica, Vatican City, October 2, 2005, Vatican website, https://www.vatican.va/content/benedict-xvi/en/homilies/2005/documents/hf_ben-xvi_hom_20051002_opening-synod-bishops.html.

3. Francis, "Message of His Holiness Pope Francis for the 35th World Youth Day 2020," February 11, 2020, Vatican website, https://www.vatican.va/content/francesco/en/messages/youth/documents/papa-francesco_20200211_messaggio-giovani_2020.html.

4. Gregory, *Dialogues*, trans. Odo John Zimmerman (New York: Newman Press, 1959), 174.

Jesus, I Worship You. Thanks for the Abundant Life: The Last 10 Days

1. Margaret Mary Alacoque, *The Autobiography of Saint Margaret Mary*, trans. Mary Philip (Gastonia, NC: TAN Books, 1995), 42.

2. Francis, "Address of Holy Father Francis," St. Peter's Square, October 12, 2013, Vatican website, https://www.vatican.va/content/francesco/en/speeches/2013/october/documents/papa-francesco_20131012_preghiera-mariana.html.

3. John Paul II, *Salvifici Doloris* (*On the Christian Meaning of Human Suffering*), Vatican website, February 11, 1984, sec. 19, https://www.vatican.va/content/john-paul-ii/en/apost_letters/1984/documents/hf_jp-ii_apl_11021984_salvifici-doloris.html.

4. John Paul II, *Salvifici Doloris*, sec. 27.

BIBLIOGRAPHY

Alacoque, Margaret Mary. *The Autobiography of Saint Margaret Mary*. Translated by Mary Philip. Gastonia, NC: TAN Books, 1995.

Aquinas, Thomas. *Summa Theologiae*. Translated by the Fathers of the English Dominican Province. Notre Dame, IN: Christian Classics, 1981.

Augustine. *The Confessions*. Translated by Maria Boulding. Hyde Park, NY: Ignatius Press, 2001.

Barron, Robert. "Bishop Barron on How to Read the Bible." Bishop Robert Barron, April 11, 2011. YouTube video, 7:39. https://www.youtube.com/watch?v=Ha5flTRTZWY&t=7s.

Benedict XVI. "General Audience." Castel Gandolfo, Italy, August 10, 2011. https://www.vatican.va/content/benedict-xvi/en/audiences/2011/documents/hf_ben-xvi_aud_20110810.html.

Benedict XVI. "Homily of His Holiness Benedict XVI." Vatican Basilica, Vatican City, October 2, 2005. https://www.vatican.va/content/benedict-xvi/en/homilies/2005/documents/hf_ben-xvi_hom_20051002_opening-synod-bishops.html.

Benedict XVI. *Sacramentum Caritatis* (*On the Eucharist as the Source and Summit of the Church's Life and Mission*). Vatican website, February 22, 2007. https://www.vatican.va/content/benedict-xvi/en/apost_exhortations/documents/hf_ben-xvi_exh_20070222_sacramentum-caritatis.html.

Brown, Brené. *The Gifts of Imperfection: Let Go of Who You Think You're Supposed to Be and Embrace Who You Are.* Center City, MN: Hazelden, 2010.

Clear, James. *Atomic Habits: An Easy and Proven Way to Build Good Habits and Break Bad Ones.* New York: Avery, 2018.

Coyle, Daniel. *The Talent Code: Greatness Isn't Born. It's Grown. Here's How.* New York: Bantam Books, 2009.

Evert, Jason. "Keynote Day 4." FOCUS Seek Conference, St. Louis Convention Center, St. Louis, Missouri, January 6, 2023.

Francis. "Address of His Holiness Pope Francis to Participants in the General Chapters of the Order of the Most Holy Savior of Saint Bridget and the Comboni Missionary Sisters." Speech, October 22, 2022. Vatican website. https://www.vatican.va/content/francesco/en/speeches/2022/october/documents/20221022-capitoli-generali.html.

Francis. "Address of Holy Father Francis." St. Peter's Square, October 12, 2013. Vatican website. https://www.vatican.va/content/francesco/en/speeches/2013/october/documents/papa-francesco_20131012_preghiera-mariana.html.

Francis. *Homily at the Eucharistic Congress.* Eucharistic Congress, Cebu City, Philippines, 2018.

Francis. "Homily for XXXVII World Youth Day." Lisbon, Portugal, August 2, 2023. Vatican website. https://www.vatican.va/content/francesco/en/homilies/2023/documents/20230802-portogallo-omelia.html.

Francis. "Message of His Holiness Pope Francis for the 35th World Youth Day." February 11, 2020. Vatican website. https://www.vatican.va/content/francesco/en/messages/youth/documents/papa-francesco_20200211_messaggio-giovani_2020.html.

Giacomelli, Rebecca Konyndyk. *Glittering Vices: A New Look at the Seven Deadly Sins and Their Remedies.* Ada, MI: Baker Academic, 2009.

Grabmann, Martin. *The Interior Life of St. Thomas Aquinas.* Milwaukee, WI: Bruce Publishing Company, 1951.

Gregory. *Dialogues.* Translated by Odo John Zimmerman. New York: Newman Press, 1959.

John Paul II. *Ecclesia de Eucharistia* (*On the Eucharist and Its Relationship to the Church*). April 17, 2023. Vatican website. https://www.vatican.va/content/john-paul-ii/en/encyclicals/documents/hf_jp-ii_enc_20030417_eccl-de-euch.html.

John Paul II. *Salvifici Doloris* (*On the Christian Meaning of Human Suffering*). February 11, 1984. Vatican website. https://www.vatican.va/content/john-paul-ii/en/apost_letters/1984/documents/hf_jp-ii_apl_11021984_salvifici-doloris.html.

Johnston, Joe, dir. *Captain America: The First Avenger.* Burbank, CA: Marvel Studios, 2011.

Liguori, Alphonsus. *Visits to the Blessed Sacrament.* Charlotte, NC: TAN Books, 2001.

McLean Hospital. "The Social Dilemma: Social Media and Your Mental Health." McLeanHospital.org, January 18, 2023. https://www.mcleanhospital.org/essential/it-or-not-social-medias-affecting-your-mental-health.

Pascal, Blaise. *Pensées.* Translated by A. J. Krailsheimer. New York: Penguin Classics, 1995.

Royal Society for Public Health. *#StatusOfMind: Social Media and Young People's Mental Health and Wellbeing.* May 2017. https://www.rsph.org.uk/our-work/campaigns/status-of-mind.html.

Sarah, Robert. *The Power of Silence: Against the Dictatorship of Noise.* San Francisco: Ignatius Press, 2017.

Scott, Ridley, dir. *The Martian.* Lost Angeles: Twentieth Century Fox, 2015.

Sheen, Fulton J. *Treasure in Clay: The Autobiography of Fulton J. Sheen.* New York: Image, 1982.

60 Minutes. "Tom Brady on Winning: There's 'Got to Be More Than This.'" January 30, 2019. YouTube video, 1:08. https://www.youtube.com/watch?v=-TA4_fVkv3c.

Sutton, Jeremy. "5 Benefits of Journaling for Mental Health." PositivePsychology.com, February 9, 2023. https://positivepsychology.com/benefits-of-journaling.

Thérèse of Lisieux. *Story of a Soul: The Autobiography of St. Thérèse of Lisieux.* Translated by John Clarke. Washington, DC: ICS Publications, 1996.

Fr. Tim Anastos is a priest of the Archdiocese of Chicago and the assistant chaplain at the St. John Paul II Newman Center at the University of Illinois–Chicago. He serves as a eucharistic preacher for the United States Conference of Catholic Bishops. Fr. Tim earned a bachelor's degree in linguistics from the University of Illinois and a bachelor's degree in sacred theology from the Pontifical University of St. Thomas Aquinas in Rome. He previously served as parochial vicar of Mary, Seat of Wisdom Parish in Park Ridge, Illinois. Fr. Tim releases *Reel Homilies*, one-minute reflections on the Sunday Mass readings through the lens of Church tradition, pop culture, and self-improvement with Spirit Juice Studios.

www.instagram.com/spiritjuice

www.tiktok.com/@spiritjuice

www.youtube.com/@SpiritJuice/shorts

The Most Rev. Andrew Cozzens, formerly archbishop of the Archdiocese of Saint Paul and Minneapolis, is bishop of the Diocese of Crookston and chairman of the board of the 2024 Eucharistic Revival Congress, as well as chairman of the USCCB Committee on Evangelization and Catechesis.

AVE
AVE MARIA PRESS

Founded in 1865, Ave Maria Press,
a ministry of the Congregation of
Holy Cross, is a Catholic publishing
company that serves the spiritual and
formative needs of the Church and its
schools, institutions, and ministers;
Christian individuals and families; and
others seeking spiritual nourishment.

For a complete listing of titles from

Ave Maria Press

Sorin Books

Forest of Peace

Christian Classics

visit www.avemariapress.com

AVE MARIA PRESS
Notre Dame, IN
A Ministry of the United States Province of Holy Cross